W9-BLR-974

The Comfortable Home

The Comfortable Home

HOW TO INVEST IN YOUR NEST AND LIVE WELL FOR LESS

MITCHELL GOLD AND BOB WILLIAMS
WITH MINDY DRUCKER

Clarkson Potter/Publishers
New York

**MELCHER
MEDIA**

Copyright © 2009 by Mitchell Gold and Bob Williams

All rights reserved.
Published in the United States by Clarkson Potter Publishers,
an imprint of the Crown Publishing Group, a division of
Random House, Inc., New York.
www.crownpublishing.com
www.clarksonpotter.com

CLARKSON POTTER is a trademark and POTTER with
colophon is a registered trademark of Random House, Inc.

This book was produced by
Melcher Media
124 West 13th Street
New York, NY 10011
www.melcher.com

Publisher: Charles Melcher
Associate Publisher: Bonnie Eldon
Editor in Chief: Duncan Bock
Executive Editor and Project Manager: Lia Ronnen
Project Editor: Lindsey Stanberry
Production Director: Kurt Andrews

Designed by Naomi Mizusaki

Library of Congress Cataloging-in-Publication Data

Gold, Mitchell.
The comfortable home : how to invest in your nest and live well
for less /
Mitchell Gold and Bob Williams.
    p. cm.
 Includes index.
 ISBN 978-0-307-58878-4
1. Interior decoration. I. Williams, Bob. II. Title.
NK2113.G645 2009   747--dc22
2009027786l

Printed in China

10 9 8 7 6 5 4 3 2 1

First Edition

DEDICATION

We got Lulu on a Monday evening. She was the runt of the litter and simply captured our hearts at first sight. The next morning, we drove her to work and called a meeting with everyone in the office. We introduced her and explained that she'd be coming to work every day, and that there was just one rule: "No people food."

Lulu went to work almost every day regardless of whether or not we were in town. She brought a spirit of unconditional love and fun to our factory and to our office employees, daycare kids, and suppliers. Lulu toured the country visiting our customers' stores, as well as the editorial offices of most of the major shelter magazines in America, and spread her joy there as well.

We think we gave Lulu an incredible life. We know Lulu gave us one.

Lulu Williams-Gold
1995–2007

CONTENTS

WE WANT TO HELP

This year we're celebrating the twentieth anniversary of Mitchell Gold + Bob Williams, the home furnishings company we founded in 1989. And after two amazing decades, it's still comfort, in every sense of the word, that's at the heart of everything we do. So we wrote *The Comfortable Home* to share with you what we've learned about achieving it, and all the wonderful ways it can improve your life.

We also wrote this book to help you save money. We believe the current economy has changed the way we'll live for a long time—consuming conspicuously has now taken a backseat to being smart about money. But one thing hasn't changed—your home is still an incredibly smart investment. Creating a beautiful, calming, and organized haven truly has the power to change your life. And the good news is that improvements can be made on any budget. It's about investing in a few great pieces rather than buying many mediocre ones. It's about decorating with items that have personal meaning no matter what the cost—and displaying them in ways that make them look like they cost more than they did.

It's also about living in a house that's "finished." Not that we're ever actually "decorated"—in fact, we deliberately design our spaces so they don't feel frozen in time. However, when you still have stuff in boxes, or bare white walls, or furniture in the same spot where the movers left it—you always feel a little unsettled. The psychological effect of a home that makes you feel good and ready for family and friends can give you energy that will benefit all areas of your life. *The Comfortable Home* offers ideas on how to make that happen.

Our advice can help you create a new home from scratch or update just a few rooms. It will guide you in buying new furnishings or incorporating pieces you already own. And best of all, our advice is appropriate for a range of home types: If you live in an apartment, your living room may be your primary living space, but if you live in a suburban house, you may use your living room primarily for entertaining. There are ideas here for both.

HOW TO USE THIS BOOK

The first chapter helps you get in touch with what you like and need. It also introduces you to our simple yet effective approaches to color, furniture arrangement, and accessorizing. From our experience, we can tell you that doing the prep work—thinking about how you want a room to function or properly measuring your space—will make decorating easier and buying furniture less intimidating.

Next are room-by-room chapters that you can use whether you are focusing on one room or decorating the entire house. But each chapter contains advice you can use no matter what you are decorating: For instance, you may find something in the Living Room chapter that might work in your family room, or a Small Space suggestion that could benefit your entryway. And interspersed with those chapters are tours of several homes—including our own New York apartment—that offer "live" examples of decorating ideas we love.

The Comfortable Home is not a catalog. In fact, we wrote the book in order to provide the kind of in-depth guidance that we can't give in our catalogs or through our retail stores. And although these pages contain many of our furnishings, we use them here to explain how that type of piece can contribute to a great décor. While some of the pieces are available for purchase, you should use those not available as inspiration to find others with similar characteristics.

WHO WE ARE

We believe that people want to know whom they're getting advice from and prefer to do business with a company that shares their core beliefs. Here are insights into how we started, where we stand, and our hopes for the future.

OUR MOTHERS MADE US DO THIS: The way we were raised had a big impact on the way we decorate. Children weren't allowed in the living room at Mitchell's house—hence his desire to make every room accessible for all. Yet his parents were always gracious hosts, and he credits them with inspiring him to make a home truly welcoming. Bob's dad was in the military, and his family moved often; he admired his mother's commitment to making each home comfortable and shares her love of antiques and collecting.

WE'RE COUNTRY FOLK AT HEART: Our company started in a small factory in Taylorsville, North Carolina, with an office in a trailer in the middle of a cow field. Today we have a state-of-the-art factory just a few miles down the road—as well as a growing number of Mitchell Gold + Bob Williams Signature Stores across the country and around the world. The many wonderful and talented people who make and sell our furniture have truly been key to our company's success.

EARLY DAYS: Mitchell, age 13, with brother Richard, whose good taste influenced Mitchell at an early age. Bob, age 6, with sister Melissa, in a tasteful owl costume, foreshadowing how design-smart he'd someday be.

TOP: Mitchell Gold + Bob Williams company family and friends at the groundbreaking ceremony for our new factory in 1998.

MIDDLE LEFT: Furniture-making in progress in the completed state-of-the-art facility in North Carolina.

MIDDLE RIGHT: The welcoming entrance to Lulu's Child Enrichment Center, our on-site daycare.

RIGHT: A group portrait of some of the center's adorable attendees and their wonderful caregivers.

WE HAVE SEVENTY-SEVEN CHILDREN: Of all the things we've done, our on-site, not-for-profit, education-based day-care center is probably what we're proudest of. It serves the children of our employees as well as members of our community. Our hope is that it will inspire other companies to do the same.

OUR DOG GUIDED MANY OF OUR DECISIONS: We've dedicated this book to Lulu, our beloved English bulldog and company mascot, who passed away in 2007. Over the years, she appeared in many of our ads and was a big hit with our customers. As one of our employees put it, "That dog sure sold a lot of furniture." But perhaps most important, she, like all dogs, instinctually understood comfort. Watching her go through her day looking for what made her feel good—from a soft chair for napping to a belly rub—was a big influence on us.

WE ALSO TAKE ADVICE FROM KIDS: We design for people who have children—and for people who have children over. We noticed that little kids have little legs, and when they're sitting on a sofa, their shoes can get it dirty—hence our love of easy-care slipcovers. And little kids like to touch things, so we thought a lot about ways to decorate that would let parents spend the least amount of time saying, "No, no, no!"

WE'RE SURE "FAMILY VALUES" ARE FOR ALL FAMILIES: Gay or straight, single-parent or multigenerational…If you stood outside our day-care center at drop-off time, you would see exactly what we're talking about. It's clearly all about love. Our goal has been to create company benefits that make families' lives easier: In addition to the day-care center, we offer a college scholarship program, a chef-run café, an annual health fair, a gym, and concierge services.

WE WEREN'T BORN "GREEN" YESTERDAY: We've been making environmentally intelligent decisions since our inception, from how we manufacture to how we pack to how we create classic, fine-quality furniture designed to be treasured over many years.

WE'VE DONE THIS BEFORE: This is our second decorating book, and in traveling around the country to do signings for our first book, *Let's Get Comfortable*, we learned a lot—from you. We got requests for more floor plans and more step-by-step guides, both of which you'll find here. We look forward to seeing and hearing from you again on our next tour; please visit our website, mgbwhome.com, to find out when we'll be in your area.

We started our company in an economic downturn and have been cost-conscious from the beginning, ensuring that what we make is a real value and how we decorate is flexible enough to accommodate life's changes. In the "thankfully, some things never change" category, however, we reprint this quote from Mitchell, which has long graced our company coffee mugs:

"When a home is successfully furnished, just walking in the door is like getting a hug."

That's what we wish for you daily.

Mitchell Gold

Bob Williams

CHAPTER 1

WHERE TO BEGIN

What is the key to smart investing in your home? We have one word for you: *planning*. It will, of course, save you time and money, and it's always easier and more affordable to get things right the first time. But more than that, proper planning will help turn a house into a sanctuary, a place where you'll want to spend your time. And if a well-decorated house results in your being at home more—whether you are entertaining, eating in, or simply enjoying your living space—that can be a benefit to you in any economy.

For us, planning begins with thinking about how you live and what changes could be made to your home to make your life run more smoothly. Then you need to figure out how to make these changes, affordably and in a style that feels natural to you. This isn't a process you'll go through just once, however. To be truly satisfying, your home needs to evolve along with your life, and we believe that flexibility should be part of your decorating plans from the beginning.

In many ways, even though we've written two decorating books, designed several houses, and are celebrating twenty years in the home-furnishings business together, we're always just starting out. Each new update is a chance to reassess what makes us feel at home. Here are some of the simple steps we use to get there.

THINK ABOUT FUNCTION

Decorating is much easier if you consider how each room will be used before you even begin to pick furniture. Rather than focusing on aesthetics, you should determine what activities you will be doing in a particular room (watching TV, entertaining guests, relaxing with a good book). This will provide a clearer sense of what you need to meet those goals.

MAKE A LIST

List all the activities you plan to do in each room. We know from experience this is the best way to get what you need to feel comfortable the first time around. Many people find decorating stressful, and list-making helps ease the pressure. You don't need a good eye or in-depth design knowledge to get the project moving. Keep these points in mind as you write your list:

- **THINK ABOUT HOW YOU'LL USE THE ROOM.** You'll get a sense of what features each piece of furniture needs to meet your goals. Do you require extra storage? Will you be using the room as a guest room? Will you be entertaining a crowd?

- **CONSIDER WHO WILL USE THE ROOM.** For true harmony, ask all members of your household to contribute to your list. Don't overlook the youngest members, who are often especially tuned in to comfort. And don't forget the needs of four-legged family members.

- **READ THE FOLLOWING ROOM-BY-ROOM CHAPTERS** for more ideas on choosing layouts and furnishings based not only on what you like visually but on how you want to live in a particular room.

It's worth taking the time to make lists for all your rooms, even those you're not currently ready to update. That way, while you're working on one room, you might find something that would enhance the usefulness of another.

BECOME FAMILIAR WITH YOUR SPACE

Snap a few pictures of your room or create a rough floor plan, with marks for windows, doors, and other architectural elements, like fireplaces. Ask yourself the following questions before you begin decorating:

- **WHAT ARE THE ROOM'S BEST FEATURES?** A beautiful view or a great fireplace? Or maybe both? Consider a seating arrangement that will let you enjoy these details.

- **WHAT'S THE FIRST THING YOU WANT PEOPLE TO SEE WHEN THEY ENTER THE ROOM?** Stand in each doorway and think about what should take center stage. Maybe it should be an inviting sofa that encourages relaxing. Or maybe it's a favorite piece of art that sets the color tone.

- **WHAT WOULD HELP TRAFFIC FLOW THROUGH THE ROOM?** The goal is to arrange the furniture so that you can move from one side of the room to another—or to another room—without walking between two people talking. One way is to position furniture away from the walls, thus creating walkways around the perimeter that allow people to avoid the conversation area.

DON'T FORGET TO MEASURE

Note the dimensions of your room, including ceiling height and all architectural elements, such as windows, doorways, and fireplaces. You'll need these to plan, shop, and talk with any design professionals or home furnishings store personnel you may consult. It's also your best assurance that you'll end up with furnishings that fit your space.

- **MAKE THE MEASUREMENTS SPECIFIC.** How big are your doorways? What's the distance from your windowsill to the floor? How much room is on either side of the fireplace? Precise measurements are important to ensure the pieces you purchase fit perfectly.

- **KEEP THE MEASUREMENTS WITH YOU AT ALL TIMES.** Stash them in your personal organizer or keep a notebook in your glove compartment or handbag. You never know when you'll see a piece you love.

COLLECT LOOKS YOU LOVE

No matter where you are in the decorating process, it's never too soon or too late to begin collecting inspiration—from books and magazines, from TV and the Internet, or even while eating at a favorite restaurant. Believe us, this isn't just for designers. It lets you see if your choices hold up as things you love over time, and it reveals patterns in what appeals to you.

For us, gathering inspiration is a way of life. When we travel—heck, even when we go to the grocery store—we see things that inspire us, from an arrangement of chairs in a hotel lobby to the colors of vegetables in the produce aisle. We'll take a picture, make a note, or do a quick sketch. Doing this helps keep you clued in to the colors, styles, and spaces that make you feel good. Keep the following steps in mind when you begin your inspiration research.

STEP 1: DO YOUR HOMEWORK

Scan books, magazines, design blogs, and other websites regularly. One of our favorite pastimes is to take a stack of magazines and some straw baskets, pull out pages, and file them in different ways: one basket for layout ideas, another for color, and another for items we'd love to own. You could also consider organizing by each room in the house. Label the baskets and go through them from time to time.

Do the same thing online, saving images to print out and add to your baskets. Use the pictures to study how professional photo stylists arrange accessories and furniture to give rooms a finished look. Don't forget to bring this inspiration with you when you shop.

Also pay attention to the furnishings in movies and on TV. Set designers have used our furniture to convey comfort and style in such shows as *CSI* and *Friends*.

STEP 2: GET OUTSIDE

It pays to do more than two-dimensional research. The world around you holds limitless possibilities: a hotel, one of our stores (we couldn't resist!), or a restaurant. Are the colors or lighting adding to your enjoyment? Are the chairs comfortable? What are the place settings like?

Find home furnishings stores that you like not only for their merchandise but also for the way the merchandise is displayed and the overall look and feel of the store itself. This may lead to inspiration for the look of your home, and it can increase the odds of finding a like-minded salesperson who can really help you with decision-making. Once there, consider the arrangements you gravitate toward. That may lead you to furnishings you might not have considered otherwise.

Friends' homes can also be a great source of ideas. What makes you feel welcome? What is special about their living spaces? What doesn't work?

STEP 3: WRITE DOWN WHAT MOVES YOU

Keep all of your notes in your organizer or start a design notebook. Snap pictures where possible (asking first). It's always great to look at your pictures at home, right in the rooms you'll be decorating.

Designate a box for paint chips, fabric swatches, and wood samples. Small found or purchased objects that express your style (a picture frame or collectible, for instance) can be great inspiration as well.

MIX AND MATCH

Most people find that they are attracted to a number of styles, rather than picking one style like modern or country and keeping everything within that look. We love this approach to decorating. For us, it's all about the mix, whether you're filling your traditional home with modern furniture or adding elements of country style to a mostly modern living room. Don't be afraid to consider furnishings from different eras with a subtle blend of finishes, fabrics, and colors. The result will be a uniquely personal space.

Sometimes, however, a home's contemporary design makes you want furnishings with a modern bent, or a marvelous memory leaves you craving the warmth of a country home like your grandmother's. Even within these style categories, you can create your own combinations. Here are three of our favorite styles.

SOFT AND MODERN

This look is defined by comfort and clean lines. Here's how to get it:

- Use only a few colors in a room, and make them mainly serene and subtle ones.
- Create richness with a variety of materials, such as wood, metal, and glass.
- Select upholstery that is soft to the touch.
- If you include pattern, pick only one, and put it on pillows, a rug, or an accent chair. Don't use it to upholster the sofa.
- Add some curves: a round side table, an oval coffee table ottoman, or a circular mirror offer a nice contrast to all the straight lines.
- Warm up the room with a collection of family photos in simple frames.

HIP TRADITIONAL

It takes only a few twists to update traditional style:

- Choose furnishings with classic shapes and modern details: a camelback sofa with sleek tapered legs instead of the traditional straight ones; a chest with drawer pulls in polished nickel instead of antique brass; or a pedestal table in a bright-colored lacquered finish.
- Use solid-colored fabrics on traditional pieces, such as an English-arm sofa in crisp linen versus a stripe.
- Install a clean-lined modern light fixture over a traditional dining table.

MODERN COTTAGE

This is definitely not your mother's country style. Here are tips to get a lighter, easier-to-care-for version that can be a great showcase for antiques and collectibles:

- Limit the number of elements and colors in the room so that vintage pieces look sculptural.
- Same goes for accessories—keep displays to a minimum to give the room a cleaner, more modern aesthetic.
- Paint one wall a happy shade, like an apple green, to introduce a punch of color that will look great as a backdrop for furnishings like soft, cushy white-slipcovered chairs and flea-market finds in distressed woods.

ADVICE ON GETTING STARTED

To keep from feeling overwhelmed—mentally, physically, or financially—figure out the order in which you'd like to get rooms done. Now is a good time to review the lists you made at the beginning of this chapter. This will give you an idea of the most beneficial place to spend your time and resources, and help you determine what furniture you need to purchase to meet your goals.

The best planning includes short- and long-term budgeting. The total cost of decorating will depend on many factors, of course, including how much you'll do yourself, how many new pieces you need, the size of your home, and so on.

It's also important to consider how redecorating might disrupt your family's routines. Certain jobs, like refinishing floors, might mean moving out for a few days; others, like kitchen renovations, may mean eating takeout for a while.

Starting with a clean slate can be very different from updating a home where you've lived for several years. Here is some more advice on getting started.

Are you moving into a new home and starting with a clean slate? Consider the following:

- **IF YOUR BUDGET ALLOWS,** rather than decorating one or two rooms completely, first set up each room's essentials. There are a few advantages to working this way. It will make your home more comfortable overall fairly quickly. It can give you energy and a sense of organization, and lets your home start to serve its vital function as a chaos-free place to take a break from the outside world. It can also allow you to collect additional pieces slowly over time.

- **IF FAMILY AND FRIENDS ALWAYS GATHER AT YOUR HOUSE,** make life easier by completing the public rooms used for entertaining first, so you're not always rushing around at the last minute trying to get things cleaned up and ready.

- **NO MATTER WHICH ROOM YOU START WITH,** avoid using any room—even private spaces like your bedroom or office—as storage space for things you don't know what to do with or want to hide when company visits. It's so hard to get a room reorganized once it becomes cluttered, and you won't be using your home to the fullest.

- **CONSIDER THE HOUSE AS A WHOLE.** Check out the Secret to Serenity section on page 22 before you begin. We find it relaxing when a home has a cohesive overall feel to it, with no jarring changes of color or style from room to room.

ROOMS TO UPDATE

If you're updating individual rooms, decide which one will be best to start with:

- **WHICH ROOM NEEDS THE LEAST WORK?** Get inspired by your success as you move forward.

- **WHICH ROOM NEEDS THE MOST WORK?** Sometimes it's good to put the most challenging work behind you.

- **THINK ABOUT THE MASTER BEDROOM.** It is important to have a relaxing and revitalizing place to escape to while the rest of the house is being redecorated.

- **IF YOU PLAN TO TACKLE MORE THAN ONE ROOM AT ONCE,** consider how to minimize disruptions of your daily life—perhaps choose one public room, such as a family room (leaving the kitchen and perhaps the living room as space for congregating), and one private room, such as a child's bedroom or home office.

HOW TO SMARTLY EMPLOY YOUR FUNDS

Divide your lists of what's needed for each room into four parts:

- **INSTANT GRATIFICATION:** These are the things you can do quickly without spending a lot of money to make the room more livable and beautiful. Maybe it's buying a new duvet and pillows for your bed. Maybe it's painting one wall to add a pop of color to the kitchen or replacing all of your standard light switches with dimmers.

- **NECESSITIES:** These are things that really must be upgraded, such as floors that should be refinished, a sofa that needs to be reupholstered or replaced, or windows that require coverings.

- **INVESTMENTS:** These are quality, more expensive pieces or renovations that will make a big difference in your life, such as a dining table that will let you entertain the way you've always wanted, or built-in shelves so that you can finally display the china you've been storing in boxes.

- **INDULGENCES YOU WON'T REGRET:** New, high-quality towels—and new terry robes to match, while you're at it.

IMPORTANT THINGS TO REMEMBER

- Let go. Our advice is to be ruthless when deciding what to keep and what to get rid of. The main difference between what you see in home-decorating magazines and what you see in many actual homes is the amount of clutter. Many homes are too cluttered. You can store some accessories and then update your rooms by changing what you display with the seasons.

- Assess what you have. If you love a piece but are changing a room so that it no longer fits there, find another room that could benefit from its presence.

- Give any unwanted items to a family member, friend, or charity—we like to give to shelters for teenagers.

THE SECRET TO SERENITY

A cohesively decorated house creates a sense of calm and harmony. When you walk into a home and feel an overall sense of well-being, what you're often responding to is the graceful flow of one room into another. By using the same, or similar, architectural details, colors, window treatments, flooring, and sometimes furnishings throughout the house, you can achieve this feeling.

This requires paying careful attention to what you can see from one room to the next. In an open-plan living and dining area, the need for a connection is clear. However, this philosophy extends even to rooms separated by narrow doorways. Here are some ways to achieve an air of serenity in your home.

WINDOW TREATMENTS

Bare windows can make a house feel unfinished, but mismatched draperies can be just as bad.

- The same simple drapes or shades hung with the same hardware throughout give a clean look.

- In a larger home, if we vary hardware and treatments because of a window's unique shape, we'll opt for similar styles in similar colors or fabrics.

COLOR

Whether you have a new home or are updating your current one, color is an affordable and effective way to bring a sense of unity.

- Keep your color choices soft. A neutral palette promotes harmony among spaces.

- Limit the number of colors in your home overall, just as you do in individual rooms. This will up the serenity factor. As a rule of thumb, use no more than three or four colors, with at least two being accents.

- You can, however, create eye-pleasing variety by changing the amount of each color in a room. For instance, taupe might be the main color in one room and then serve as an accent in another where creams and beiges dominate. Turn the page for more on our color philosophy.

ARCHITECTURAL DETAILS

Consistency is essential for achieving cohesiveness:

- Paint or finish all wood trim in the same way.

- You might want to add trim if your home doesn't come with it. It can go a long way toward making a room look finished.

- Use the same style, finish, and color for your doors and hardware.

- Keep the flooring consistent. Different floor colors or finishes in hallways and adjacent rooms can make a layout feel choppy.

OUR COLOR PHILOSOPHY

Your home should be a sanctuary, and color can help you reach this goal. The right color can be relaxing and rejuvenating, and can give a room great energy. We have two rules for how to use color: 1) Stick mostly with solids and 2) use only three or four colors in a room, with at least two being accent colors. There are so many elements in a room—art, rugs, architectural details, upholstery, accessories, photographs—and too many competing colors can make a space feel unsettled.

We also prefer colors that are soft and soothing. A stronger or brighter color works best when used sparingly, as a carefully placed accent in a neutral setting.

We often consider the principles of the color wheel when choosing hues. We gravitate toward secondary colors, formed from the combination of two primaries (pure red, blue, or yellow), or the tertiaries, a blend of the three primaries or a primary plus a secondary. We believe that a toned-down palette is more relaxing. Our color schemes also combine hues that are close to each other on the color wheel. This adds to the serenity of the room because the colors aren't jarring to the eye.

You'd be amazed at how the addition of color can change your room for the better, often quickly and affordably. Color can:

- **BECOME A FOCAL POINT** in a room that doesn't have any special architectural features. For instance, you might paint one wall a strong hue and put a favorite piece of furniture you'd like to highlight against it to draw attention to that piece.

- **MAKE A ROOM FEEL LARGER.** Lighter shades of cooler colors—blues, grays, greens, lavenders—can make a room seem larger. Cooler versions of whites and creams can achieve a similar goal.

- **MAKE A ROOM FEEL COZIER.** Darker shades and warmer hues—beiges, yellows, oranges, reds—can make a space feel more intimate.

- **CHANGE THE PERCEPTION OF HEIGHT.** Painting a ceiling white or a light color will make it feel higher, while a darker or richer color will appear to lower it.

- **DIVIDE A ROOM.** In an open-plan living/dining area, you can set off the different spaces by painting the dining area a few shades darker than the same color and creating the feeling of two rooms.

OPPOSITE: This off-white room really comes alive with one wall painted persimmon.

OUR FAVORITE COLOR COMBINATIONS

There are certain colors that just make you feel good—when you see them, you smile. We call them our happy colors. They include raspberry, apple green, and sky blue. These are great accent colors for rooms primarily decorated in shades of white or taupe. Since these colors could easily be overwhelming, we like to use one per room—say, raspberry and white or orange and taupe—not several combined.

Make sure that the color accents aren't all grouped together. If you have a brightly colored lamp, bowl, and pillow, for example, strategically place them in the room so that your eye moves comfortably from one pop of color to the next.

And don't forget to consider what makes you happy. Is there one particular color that comes up over and over again in your life? If you're always picking blue items, chances are you'll be happy living with blue.

UPHOLSTERY FABRIC COLOR CHOICES

- **STAY WITH SOLID COLORS** for major pieces. This will make it easier for you to give them—and your whole room—a new look by changing pillows, throws, or rugs.

- **IF YOU LIKE OPTIONS,** go with slipcovered pieces. A second set of slipcovers in another color and fabric lets you freshen a room when the seasons change or whenever you want a new look.

- **IF YOU'RE CONCERNED ABOUT DIRT AND GENERAL WEAR AND TEAR,** a good choice is a fabric that appears solid but has texture and color variation, such as a tweed.

- **IF YOU WANT A LIGHT-COLORED SOLID FABRIC,** you'll appreciate the benefits of performance fabrics. Available as faux suedes, wovens, or textures, they are durable and stain resistant. Although they are synthetic, they're long-lasting and can clean up with soap and water.

ADDING POP WITH PATTERN

Think about the patterns you may want to use in the beginning of the decorating process to make sure they are in keeping with the rest of your palette. Use pattern sparingly and in places where it won't feel overwhelming. Accessories or smaller pieces of furniture—such as pillows or accent chairs—are ideal. Their size is better suited to a pop of pattern, and these pieces are more affordable to replace when you're ready for a change. A rug, too, is a practical choice, because a good pattern hides dirt.

A NOTE ON NEUTRALS

We love whites, creams, and beiges with our happy colors, but soft and subtle pinks, greens, and blues can also feel like neutrals. They are best used as a room's primary color and accompanied by only one to three accent colors. Like whites and beiges, these colors will stand the test of time and won't look outdated in a few years. They can also be updated affordably. However, don't forget that wall color is a great place to experiment—it's easy to repaint if you don't like what you have.

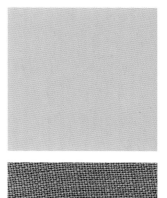

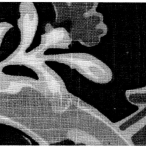

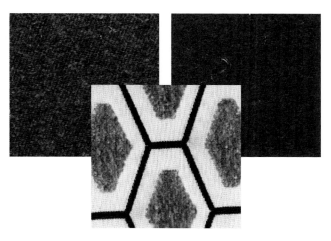

THINGS TO CONSIDER WHEN BUYING UPHOLSTERED PIECES

Don't forget to test-drive any upholstered furniture before you purchase. Many pieces of furniture may look beautiful, but we know from experience that you'll only be happy if they are also really comfortable. Here's how to determine comfort:

- Take off your coat, put down your packages, and lean back into a sofa like you would at home. A well-made sofa will have extra padding in the corners and on the arms.
- If this will be your family room sofa, the true test is to lie down. Don't be afraid to do that right in the store.
- Even if a sofa's purpose will be more formal, be sure to check its comfort by noting if the back pitch, arm height, and seat depth will suit those who will sit in it most.

THE INSIDE

Questions to ask about the things you can't see:

- **WHAT IS THE FRAME MADE OF?** Hardwoods such as maple, poplar, and ash are more durable than softwoods such as pine. Kiln drying takes the moisture out and prevents warping and mildew. Many frames include a highly durable material called engineered hardwood, made of multiple layers of thin wood glued together, that does not crack or warp.

- **HOW IS THE FRAME HELD TOGETHER?** A strong frame is secured with double dowels and/or mortise-and-tenon joints, as well as high-pressure staples, wood glue, and corner blocks screwed into place.

- **WHAT ARE THE CUSHIONS MADE OF?** Are they filled with down, a down blend (a mix of down, feathers, and fiber in a casing around a foam core), or poly (a foam core wrapped in layers of poly fiber)? Down needs the most maintenance; poly is the easiest to take care of.

- **HOW IS THE FOAM MANUFACTURED?** Environmentally friendly foam is made in a manner that releases no ozone-depleting CFCs into the atmosphere.

THE OUTSIDE

Sofas come in many shapes and coverings.

SHAPE:
- Arms: Rolled, square, English-style, or armless.
- Legs: Tapered, square, or turned; low to high; dark to light finishes.
- Skirt: Straight or with kick-pleats; touching the floor or raised up to show some leg. Many modern styles have no skirt at all.

COVERING:

- Upholstery: Fabric that is permanently attached to the frame.
- Slipcover: A removable cover designed to go over a muslin-upholstered base.

SEAT CUSHION CONFIGURATION: There are benefits to a variety of styles.

- Bench: One long cushion is good for lying down and seats three easily.
- Two-cushion: A large two-cushion sofa can seat four.
- Three-cushion: Seats three people comfortably.

CUSHION TYPE: Comfort plays a major role here.

- Loose back and seat: Lets you adjust cushions for your own comfort.
- Tight back and seat: Sleek-looking and supportive, but throw pillows are necessary if you want to curl up.
- Tight back and loose seat: The best of both worlds if you add some soft throw pillows.
- Semi-attached cushions: Attached to the frame so they stay in place while still offering that sink-in quality.

THE ORDERING PROCESS

Three terms you'll hear in a home furnishings store:

- **IN STOCK:** A piece already manufactured and waiting in a warehouse in the same fabric and size as the one you see in the store. Ask a salesperson which items are available for immediate delivery.

- **SPECIAL ORDER:** If the stock pieces won't work with your floor plan or color scheme, you can place a special order, picking your frame and fabric. This method takes longer, of course, as the piece needs to be made. Delivery time can range widely, from six weeks to six months. (We strive to deliver in six weeks.)

- **C.O.M.:** Customer's Own Material, a special-order option available at an additional charge, where you have a piece upholstered or slipcovered in material that you have purchased from another store.

THINGS TO CONSIDER WHEN BUYING WOOD FURNITURE

Quality case goods—a term the furniture industry uses for the product category that includes dining tables, consoles, buffets, and more—can be an investment, but the information provided here will help you to make a smart purchase.

Because solid wood furnishings were once part of trees, they remain "alive": In dry environments, they lose moisture and contract, which can cause loose drawers. In wet environments, they absorb moisture and swell, resulting in drawers that stick. Over time, this cycle can make solid wood warp or split.

VENEERS

Veneers, thin cuts of beautifully grained hardwoods, are a great alternative to solid wood furniture for several reasons:

- They are much easier for artisans to use. They can be as thin as 1/64 of an inch—a benefit when working on the curved front of a serpentine chest, for instance.
- They allow for the use of the rarest, finest, and most expensive grains of wood in smaller, more cost-effective doses. Some of the most beautiful patterns are called marquetry, consisting of several woods cut into intricate pieces, laid out in a pattern by hand, and then glued to the surface of a piece.
- Most veneers are glued over engineered hardwood, such as medium-density fiberboard (MDF), an extremely durable and cost-effective material made of compressed wood fibers that doesn't warp or split.

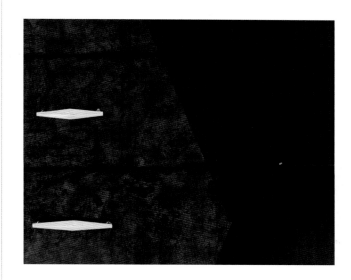

CONSTRUCTION

Look for for the following marks of high-quality case goods:

- Environmental soundness: The use of plantation-grown tropical woods, for instance.
- Uniformity: Look for one large piece of veneer rather than individual squares with misaligned grains.
- Extra effort: Even the backs of chests and undersides of tables should feel smooth.
- Fine hardware: Hardware should be custom-designed and sized well for the piece. And it should feel great to the touch. Metal hardware is made in a mold, which leaves a line where the two sides of the mold meet. On fine hardware, the line is polished smooth.
- Good drawers: Look for dovetailed (interlocking) solid wood panels on all sides (shown above); for large drawers, there should be two glides (versus one) on the bottom for smoother opening. Drawers that are painted inside are such a great surprise.

FINISH

Finishes protect the wood and help to maintain its original moisture content. They also bring out its beauty. Two factors determine how well they do this:

- Depth and clarity: "Depth" refers to how far into the wood the finish appears to go. "Clarity" refers to how visible the grain of the wood is. Lesser-quality finishes tend to be cloudier and flatter, often because they were done assembly-line style rather than by a single craftsperson.
- Touch: Quality furniture feels smooth when you run your hand over it—no rough edges.

CHOOSING THE RIGHT LIGHT

All rooms need two types of light: ambient, or general, lighting and lighting to illuminate specific areas or objects. Don't forget the following:

- You can turn every seat in the house into a potential reading area by ensuring that there's a lamp—table, standing, or overhead—nearby. Workspaces in particular need proper lighting to avoid eyestrain, as do stairs and passageways to prevent accidents.
- Give yourself as many lighting options as possible by installing dimmer switches in all the rooms. This is an easy and affordable upgrade that will let you adjust the lighting from soft for entertaining to bright for working.
- Remember the very affordable power of candles, whether they be candlestick sconces or hanging lanterns, to transform any space. Tapers, pillars, and tea lights are great to have on hand too. Add some fresh flowers and you have an elegant and easy centerpiece for the dining room whenever it's needed.
- Track lights and recessed lighting are great if you want to show off works of art. It may be worthwhile to consult with a design or lighting professional if you go this route.

TABLE AND DESK LAMPS

- Lamps can be some of your most beautiful accessories. They offer a chance to introduce color and texture into your décor.
- Make sure they are proportionate to the size of the tables they sit upon and large enough to cast sufficient light.
- Simple modern lamps can blend nicely with more traditional furniture.
- Lamps flanking a sofa or bed don't need to match, although you may want the end tables they sit on to be the same.
- Make sure lamps have a similar visual weight as the rest of your furniture. For instance, in a neutral room, a lamp with a gilt base or a bright shade will draw more attention than a beige sofa or chair.
- Revitalize lamps you already own: Get new shades in a different color, or even a new finial, the decorative screw-on top piece that holds the shade in place.

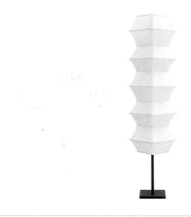

STANDING LAMPS

- This standing lamp—almost sculptural—is great for mood lighting.
- For most standing lamps, the bottom of the lamp shade should hit at about eye level for a seated person to help keep the light from shining in his or her eyes.
- An arched standing lamp provides great light over a sectional sofa.
- If your furnishings are set away from the walls, have floor outlets installed so that lamp cords don't look unsightly or become hazardous.

SCONCES

- Sconces in a dining room create an overall glow and can be used to augment the light from a chandelier.
- Sconces are a great way to evenly light a hallway. Depending on the length of the hallway, space them about 8' apart.
- Install them so that the bottom of the sconce is about 5' from the floor.
- Swing-arm styles make great adjustable reading lamps on either side of a bed.

CHANDELIERS AND PENDANTS

- These are ideal over dining tables and kitchen islands, as well as in entryways and stairwells. They can also be used over seating areas in a living room or bedroom.
- If you center a hanging lamp over your dining table, make sure that it's at least several inches narrower than the table so no one bumps it when standing up. Lamp height depends on ceiling height; hang it 30" above the table for an 8' ceiling; raise it an additional 3" for each additional foot of ceiling height.
- Use frosted bulbs if the chandelier has shades. The frosted light from them will not cast shadow lines from the metal arms on the inside of your shades.
- A duo or trio of pendant lamps with colored shades can brighten up a dining room.
- In an entryway, plan for about 7' of clearance beneath the fixture. A low-ceilinged entry will dictate the size and style of lighting you should use.
- Large, heavy chandeliers should be professionally installed.

PRETTY LITTLE THINGS

This final decorating layer is one of our favorites. When you get to this point, you can breathe a sigh of relief—the big decisions are done. However, don't lose your focus, as accessories and flowers can really change the look of a room.

FLOWER POWER

There are two very different kinds of flower arrangements. There is the kind that often comes from a florist: tall and dramatic with several kinds of flowers in different colors, and meant to be the focal point of a room. Then there's the kind we like: simple arrangements composed of one color and one variety of flower. We prefer low arrangements that don't block the view of the person sitting across from you.

- **WE LOVE WHITE FLOWERS.** Try a vase of lilies, orchids, hydrangeas, tulips, daisies, or ranunculus. A single color can be a great accent to a room, as can a simple display of greenery from your yard.

- **DIVIDE AND CONQUER:** Sometimes you'll get a bouquet with fussy filler greenery. For a more natural arrangement, keep what you like and separate it into small vases. Of course, do it after your guests depart.

- **A VASE CAN BE AN INTERESTING OBJECT IN ITS OWN RIGHT.** On the other hand, a glass cylinder or bowl allows the blooms to take center stage. Flowers also look great in repurposed containers or flea-market finds, such as a vintage mold.

ACCESSORY AID

Homes should be personalized with accessories, flea-market finds, and family photos, but we know it can be difficult to figure out how to arrange items so they enhance your home without cluttering it or detracting from its style. Here are some tips:

- **STRIVE FOR BALANCE** in your arrangement of personal objects. Spread them out around the room and make sure one end of the room doesn't feel too crowded. Yet balance doesn't have to mean symmetry— for example, you don't have to arrange objects in exactly the same way on both sides of a mantel.

- **GROUP OBJECTS TO CREATE IMPACT.** Consider combining based on color, style, or shape. Edit your groupings regularly for an easy update. Designate an accessories storage shelf or closet where you can put extra items, and rotate them seasonally or as the mood strikes.

- **CREATE A VARIETY OF HEIGHTS IN YOUR ARRANGEMENTS.** There is a reason so many accessories are sold in groups of small, medium, and large—it's pleasing to the eye. If you have two items that are the same size, raise one up with a book to create a height difference, then add a lamp that's even taller as the third item. Trios of objects also look great in circular formations: small on the right, medium on the left, tall in the middle. Then you can add a second layer of an extra-small and an extra-large item. Master threes and build the number of items in your collection from there.

HOW TO MAINTAIN YOUR FURNITURE

To us, the secret to maintaining your furniture is often just about common sense. Here, we offer basic suggestions for keeping your fabric- and leather-covered pieces—including sofas, chairs, and ottomans—as well as your case goods, like dining tables, consoles, cabinets, and buffets, looking new. The key is teaching each of your family members (and your cleaning service if you employ one) to follow our sage advice.

FABRIC AND LEATHER

- **VACUUM OR BRUSH** upholstery regularly.

- **FLUFF CUSHIONS WEEKLY.** Flip and rotate every few months for even wear and fading.

- **HAVE UPHOLSTERY PROFESSIONALLY CLEANED** every 12 to 24 months.

- **DIRECT SUN CAN CAUSE FADING.** Keep drapes or blinds closed when a room isn't in use. We know this can be a pain, but it's important.

- **IF SOMETHING HAS SPILLED,** pat the spot immediately with a soft white cloth. Don't rub—it might alter the texture of the fabric and set the stain deeper into it. Test cleaners in a hidden spot to ensure they don't ruin the upholstery.

- **CHECK IF A SLIPCOVER IS WASHABLE OR DRY-CLEANABLE** before you clean it, or it will shrink and lose its shape. Wash all pieces at once to avoid color variations. Remember that all cotton fabrics shrink about 2 percent, which might be too much for a tight slipcover. Depending on the fabric, an in-home professional cleaning service is another option.

- **DON'T USE DETERGENTS, POLISHES, OR SADDLE SOAP ON LEATHER PIECES;** they remove natural oils. Don't place leather too close to heat sources (radiators or the fireplace), as it can crack and age prematurely. Dab spills immediately with a soft white cloth dampened in lukewarm distilled (not tap) water to prevent watermarks. Some scratches can be removed over time by rubbing them with your fingertips.

WOOD FURNITURE

- **LESS IS MORE.** Do not use commercial cleaning products. Simply dust with a damp cloth and dry immediately with another soft cloth.

- **POLISH WITH NATURAL BEESWAX TWICE A YEAR.** Use wax sparingly to avoid buildup. Polishing too much can cloud the finish.

- **ALWAYS USE COASTERS.** Put felt or leather pads under lamps and accessories to prevent scratches. Never place hot objects directly on wood; use place mats, table coverings, or trivets. Blot spills immediately with a soft cloth.

- **PROTECT YOUR WOOD FURNITURE FROM THE ELEMENTS.** Avoid overexposure to sun, heat, cold, and damp or dry conditions. Position your furniture away from heating vents and open windows. Close shades or drapes to prevent fading. A humidifier or dehumidifier can be useful to regulate the amount of moisture in the air.

- **IF DRAWERS ARE DIFFICULT TO OPEN,** run a white taper candle or bar of soap over the glides.

INVEST IN QUALITY AND MOTHER EARTH

These days, everyone has a different take on being green, from incorporating energy-efficient design to choosing natural materials to recycling packing materials. To these we add three favorite suggestions (which also happen to be smart budgeting ideas!):

INCORPORATE FLEA-MARKET FINDS

Can you make successful purchases at flea markets even if you don't think you have a great eye? How do you spot what you need and know if it will work? Many people buy objects they never use because they forget the basic rules of decorating. There's one secret to success we can all practice: planning. Before hitting the flea markets, remember the following tips:

- **NOTE LOCATIONS IN YOUR HOME** that need new things, and make a shopping list of what you'd like to find. Maybe even snap some photos to take along with you.

- **WRITE DOWN ALL YOUR DIMENSIONS,** being as specific as possible—the wall space between windows, the distance between shelves in a curio cabinet.

- **BRING YOUR LIST** and a tape measure with you.

REPURPOSE

This is Bob's favorite piece of decorating advice: Find new places and uses for things you already own. It can be a great way to reconsider pieces you love and encourage yourself to give them a better place in your home. It's also a great way to add personality at absolutely no cost. Some ideas:

- **TURN AN OLD DINING TABLE** into a desk.

- **USE A FAVORITE SIDE CHAIR** as a nightstand.

- **MOVE A TALL CHEST FROM A BEDROOM** to an entryway, hall, or dining room for added storage.

- **PUT A LOW CHEST BESIDE A SOFA AS AN END TABLE.** It will double as a great display and storage space.

- **SWITCH THE SIDE TABLES** in your living room with the nightstands in your bedroom.

- **USE GLASS JARS, TINS, AND OTHER VINTAGE CONTAINERS** as vases, pencil holders, and photo storage.

CHOOSE FINE FURNISHINGS

Going green means planning ahead: Use the advice in this book to be certain that you're acquiring the right furniture. Don't be afraid to invest in the important pieces. (In the room-by-room chapters, see The Essentials for buying tips and Form + Function for ideas on which pieces have the features you need and the look you want.) Stay away from trends and choose pieces that you can imagine living with for a long time.

It also means buying environmentally sound furniture. Ask salespeople at the stores where you shop what the sofa or table you're interested in is made of. This is something we've been researching since we started our company.

Today, our sofa cushions are wrapped in 80 percent regenerated fibers and have foam that is ozone-friendly, noncarcinogenic, and composed of up to 10 percent soy, a natural renewable resource. Our frames use domestic woods that come from responsibly managed forests; the glues are water-based and biodegradable; and the metal springs are 65 percent recycled metal. Our fabrics include eco-friendly natural fibers such as cotton, hemp, linen, and mohair. Many of our case goods are made from eco-friendly parawood solids. The trees aren't harvested until they stop producing sap, thereby using our natural resources without harming the environment.

And in addition to what companies make their products from, also look for businesses devoted to keeping up with the evolving practices and changing manufacturing methods and technologies needed to stay green.

SHOULD YOU DO IT WITH A DESIGNER?

A good interior designer can tailor the guidelines in this chapter to your space. While an additional cost, a designer can save you time and money in the long run by ensuring that you get things right the first time. People are often surprised to learn that we sometimes turn to an interior designer for assistance with our own homes.

WHERE TO FIND A DESIGNER

Here are four good sources:

- **PEOPLE YOU KNOW** who have worked with a designer successfully and within similar budgets.

- **SALESPEOPLE** in home furnishings stores you like; they sometimes work in conjunction with designers and their clients.

- **BOOKS, BLOGS, MAGAZINES, AND SHOW HOUSES** that feature the work you like. Note the names of the designers, then Google them and check design blogs for reviews of their work.

- **THE AMERICAN SOCIETY OF INTERIOR DESIGNERS (ASID).** Those who meet the organization's membership requirements (including design education, full-time work experience, and a qualifying exam) can list ASID after their names.

THE INTERVIEWING PROCESS

Plan to meet with at least three designers to get a sense of how they work. You can save time by asking basic information via phone or email. Tell them about your home and what you hope to accomplish. If you love our look, tell them that. Here is a list of important questions to ask:

- Do you have experience with this type of project?
- What and how do you charge?
- Are you available now? How many other homes are you working on at the same time?
- Can you finish the project by a certain date? How long do you estimate it will take?
- Will you be comfortable working collaboratively with me?
- Are you experienced at combining things I already own with new purchases?
- How, and how often, would we be communicating during the project?
- What is your work experience and education?
- Are you a member of a professional group?

Then, either face-to-face or via email, share your visual inspirations and note how the designers respond: Do they seem truly interested? Are they asking questions to further their understanding of the project?

Perhaps most important, make sure you feel comfortable. This is vital in a relationship that may last many months and in which you'll regularly need to speak honestly about what you like and don't like.

Remember that designers will also have questions for you. For example, they'll want to know your budget, who has final say, and how long you've lived in your home and how long you plan to stay, plus personal information such as marital status and if you have children or pets.

Finally, get references, and call them—it's really worth it. Make sure the references are from recent jobs, and ask how satisfied clients were not only with the results, but also with the working relationship. Were there any surprises? How easily were differing opinions resolved? How close were they to staying on budget and on time?

BENEFITS

Designers are good for busy people—like personal trainers, they motivate you to get things done. They also often know great sources for goods and services. Other pluses include:

- **ASKING THE RIGHT QUESTIONS** to help you figure out your needs.

- **INTERPRETING** the photos from magazines you've collected and translating your preferences into your dream interiors.

- **CREATING A SHOPPING LIST WITH YOU**—what's missing, what to replace, what to keep and use in a different room.

- **COMING UP WITH A COLOR PALETTE** that will make you happy.

- **CREATING FLOOR PLANS** that make the most of your space.

- **OFFERING RESOURCES** that expand your options in goods and services.

- **SUGGESTING ALTERNATIVES** that might better fit your budget.

- **SHOPPING WITH YOU** to help determine what will fit your space.

- **MEDIATING** when two people are trying to merge their stuff into one household.

- **PROBLEM-SOLVING** for a family with conflicting needs and desires.

CONCERNS

The two biggest concerns people have about hiring a decorator are the worry of losing control and the cost. On control: Make sure you hire someone who is in sync with the design aesthetic to which you aspire. Also decide how much influence you want to exert. In the end, you have to respect your designer's work, and they have to respect that it's your home. Cost is another concern, but the good news is that designers work in many ways. Shop around for the kind of help you need: a consultation, room-by-room guidance, or advice about redecorating the whole house.

Here are three primary ways designers get paid:

- **COST PLUS:** The designer buys the materials, furnishings, and services at cost and then sells them to you at that cost plus an additional percentage for their time.

- **FLAT FEE:** An amount that covers all costs, from initial consultation to final installation, including the cost of goods if you have a preapproved budget.

- **HOURLY RATE:** This can be used for anything from an initial consultation to decorating a whole house

Some designers combine an hourly rate for consultations with a cost-plus arrangement on goods and services. In addition, some require a retainer. Ask for an estimate for the entire project and then expect to pay an additional 20 percent. The extra will be the likely result of unexpected problems, any additions or upgrades you might want, or because they underestimated the price.

If you decide a designer is not right for you, you can also find help at your local home furnishings store. Some stores offer in-home consultations—if you like both the furniture and the way the store is arranged, check with the sales staff to see if they offer this service. You can also bring your lists, photos, measurements, and floor plans to the store. In our signature stores, the sales staff is trained to help you create finished rooms but not to do all the details an interior designer does (like window coverings or bathrooms).

COST COMPARISONS

Like most people, we love fine things and memorable travels. But we are often surprised by how willing people are to buy an expensive designer handbag while they are unwilling to invest in a new piece of furniture.

If the thought of investing in new furniture raises your anxiety level, you're not alone. We've found that people sometimes spend more time agonizing over a $1,800 sofa than over a $48,000 car. Research has shown that people view decorating as stress-inducing, and to an extent, we understand. You can hide an expensive shirt that doesn't fit quite right in the back of your closet. It's not so easy to hide a sofa. But the rewards of a comfortable home are so great, especially in uncertain times, when an inviting space makes eating in, hanging out, and entertaining at home a pleasure.

What we're suggesting is reprioritizing rather than sacrificing. The choices are, of course, entirely personal; substitute your preferences for our suggestions. In the room-by-room chapters in this book, you'll also find sections called Easy Updates with a range of budget-friendly ideas for enhancing every room in your home.

THE ULTIMATE INVESTMENT: A STAYCATION INSTEAD OF A VACATION

If your family plans two weeklong vacations annually, making one a "staycation" (time spent relaxing at home rather than traveling) could free up funds to decorate a room of your home each year. Think about the cost of a week's vacation in the Caribbean for a family of five:

Transportation to airport or parking $200
5 round-trip plane tickets $2,500
   (school vacations usually fall on "blackout"
   periods, when you can't use frequent-flyer miles)
1 suite or 2 hotel rooms $3,000
   (most hotels allow only 4 to a room)
Meals $1,500
Rental car. $800
Activities for 3 kids and 2 adults $1,500
Incidentals $500
TOTAL $10,000

You could create a family room like the one below for less than $10,000.

Traveling as a family is invaluable, but don't underestimate the fun and relaxation of staying home without the burden of work and school. And if your job requires extensive travel, it's tempting to stay out of airports, sleep in your own bed, and get to know the local sights.

If you were to start this tradition while your children were young and get a room done every year, it would give them another kind of wonderful memory and a great foundation in life: a beautiful, comfortable, and well-organized home. We've seen many examples of how much children actually enjoy picking out furniture.

OTHER WAYS TO SPEND YOUR MONEY

INSTEAD OF
A $500
DESIGNER
HANDBAG... →

→
YOU COULD
HAVE A NEW
FLOOR LAMP →

INSTEAD OF
A $1,500
WATCH... →

→
YOU MIGHT
GET YOURSELF
A COMFORTABLE
ARMCHAIR →

INSTEAD OF
A WEEKEND
FOR TWO IN A
MAJOR CITY... →

→
YOU COULD
CREATE A
PERFECT SPOT
FOR RELAXING
YEAR-ROUND →

CITY NEST

A few good pictures can be worth many words when it comes to describing our style. What better way to explain it than to bring you into our home so you can see firsthand how we love to live?

We both have full-time homes in North Carolina, near the Mitchell Gold + Bob Williams factory, the heart of the furniture company we founded twenty years ago. However, we're often in New York for business. So after way too many years of staying in hotels, we decided to search for our dream home in the city. Two years ago, we found it: two apartments—one 1-bedroom and one 2-bedroom—on the fifty-eighth floor of a high-rise building in the center of Manhattan. We hired an architect and contractor to combine the two apartments and turn the space into a 2,200-square-foot apartment with two master suites and picture-perfect views of the city on three sides.

We knew we wanted the apartment to be a place for both entertaining and working when we're in the city. And the incredible views were the obvious focal point of each room. So our decorating goal became twofold: to give the apartment the same comfortable, relaxed style we enjoy in our North Carolina homes and to avoid doing anything that would upstage the skyline.

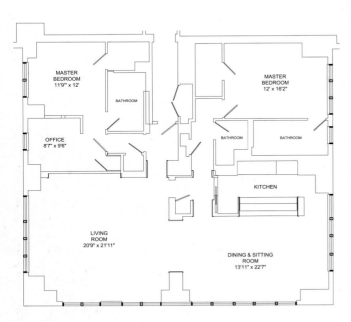

ABOVE: The square floor plan consists of an open living and dining area that's great for entertaining, plus two master suites. All the rooms have views, which were the biggest influence on our layout, color, and furnishing choices.

RIGHT: Area rugs define the dining and sitting areas near the kitchen. The color scheme here matches the rest of the apartment, creating an overall calming effect. The upholstery—like the cloud-white sofa with cerulean pillows—complements the sky and makes you feel like you're floating above the city. A good investment: the simple white sheer draperies. In addition to adding softness to the room, they help prevent overheating and furniture fading.

LEFT: We love the way the windows are low enough to let you take in the sights even when you're sitting down. The cream-colored daybed completes the conversation area without blocking the view when you're sitting on the sectional. Even the sculpture beside it is see-through. The room's colors take on different tones throughout the day as the light in the apartment changes.

FOLLOWING PAGE: The curves of the sectional are echoed in the accessories—including the globe, blue glass vases, and wooden ball sculpture—and contrast nicely with the room's otherwise straight lines. The chairs opposite the sectional nearly fade into the background as you look out at the city. The living room is entertaining-ready: A trio of iron nesting tables with stone tops serves as a side table, and the large square tufted-leather ottoman provides extra serving, seating, or display space depending on the event.

ABOVE: The tufting on a cream leather roll-back chair and the graining of a side table made from a tree trunk turned on a lathe add subtle pattern and texture without being distracting.

LEFT: A wall opposite the windows features selections from our collection of photography by Tipper Gore. Grouping the photos together over a console, and keeping much of the rest of the wall space in the room blank, calls attention to the photos and keeps them from competing with the view.

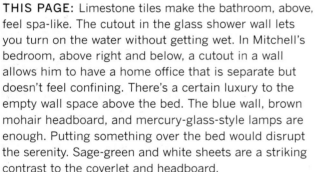

THIS PAGE: Limestone tiles make the bathroom, above, feel spa-like. The cutout in the glass shower wall lets you turn on the water without getting wet. In Mitchell's bedroom, above right and below, a cutout in a wall allows him to have a home office that is separate but doesn't feel confining. There's a certain luxury to the empty wall space above the bed. The blue wall, brown mohair headboard, and mercury-glass-style lamps are enough. Putting something over the bed would disrupt the serenity. Sage-green and white sheets are a striking contrast to the coverlet and headboard.

OPPOSITE: Needing only a laptop to do business these days makes using a beautiful desk a home-office option. A pair of slipcovered dining chairs and an étagère make the compact workspace attractive and enjoyable enough to be part of the bedroom. The chairs can be moved to the dining room for extra seating.

ABOVE: Art doesn't have to be expensive—it can just look that way. We were lucky enough to find this painting at a flea market for just $29 and put it in a simple frame.

LEFT: Bob used a wall of gathered draperies behind his bed to add color and pattern. The bedding mixes a horizontally striped fitted sheet with a white top sheet that has a vertically striped cuff. Bob prefers a daybed by the window to a desk; he likes working there on his laptop, enjoying the view. It's also a great place to pack a suitcase.

CHAPTER 2

THE ENTRYWAY

We believe in greeting guests at the door when we entertain. It sets the tone for the whole visit. By the same token, how you design your entryway can contribute to how you feel when you get home. Your entry can make your life easier, your family more organized, and your guests more comfortable. It's fun to decorate because it doesn't require a big budget or lots of stuff. And it's also ripe for repurposed items: Are there candidates among your current tables, chests, chairs, mirrors, and accessories that might fit well in this space?

THINGS TO CONSIDER

First impressions count, and your entry is no exception to that rule. Make it as organized and inviting as the rest of your home. Also, be realistic about the amount of space you have; avoid overcrowding it with furnishings or accessories so that people feel at ease passing through.

Because an entryway connects to other rooms, its furnishings should work with all the spaces visible from it. However, this doesn't preclude you from featuring a special piece—like a tall dresser passed down in the family or a pair of antique chairs. Wallpapering the wall opposite the door or painting it in an accent color is another welcoming touch.

Some of the small-space planning ideas you'll find in Chapter 7 will also come in handy here. For instance, in a compact entryway, wall space can serve decorative and practical purposes.

Here you'll find layout suggestions for several types of entryways both large and small, from long halls to simple squares to a space that runs the width of the house.

COMPACT

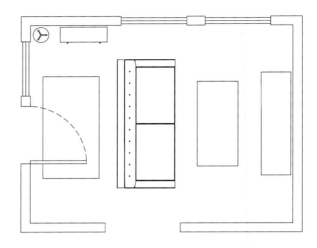

1. CARVE OUT A CORNER: Even when the front door opens right into the living room, use flooring and furnishings to establish a well-appointed entry. Add a small durable but attractive rug, a coatrack in a corner, and a console with a mirror above it by the door.

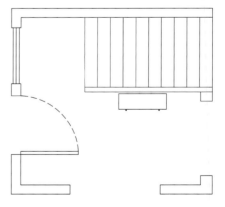

2. BORROW A VIEW: In close quarters, consider adding interesting details like an antique chest or a decorative umbrella stand by the entryway. Also think of the views into adjoining rooms as an opportunity to show your personality.

MIDSIZE

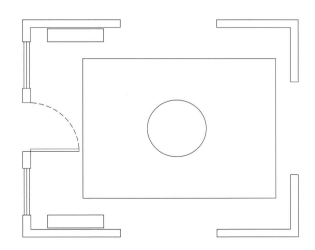

1. UPDATE A SQUARE: An icon of traditional style, the simple, symmetrical center-hall foyer—with a round table placed on a rug and topped with a chandelier—gets a convenient storage boost thanks to twin chests set on either side of the front door.

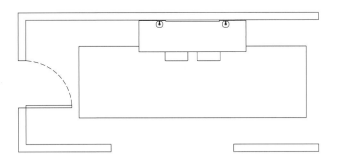

2. WARM IT UP: A runner livens up a long space and invites people inside. Upholstered cube ottomans under a console table offer more seating for company. To brighten the space, add a mirror and wall sconces. Put up family photos and let the space also serve as a gallery.

SPACIOUS

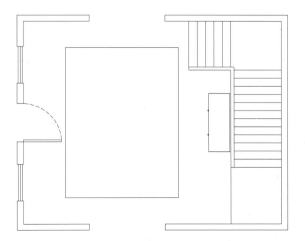

1. A BALANCED APPROACH: Keep a large entry open for greeting guests, but warm it up with a colorful rug. A beautiful chest opposite the front door is more than decorative, providing seasonal storage and a place for attractive organizers like trays and bowls.

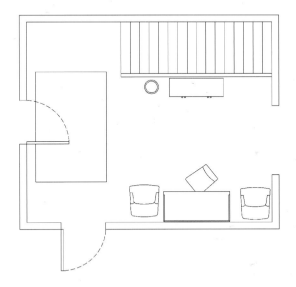

2. TWO-PART STORY: Here's an entryway that gives you everything you need right by the front door—a console, a mirror, a pair of chairs, an umbrella stand, and a coat closet—as well as a desk perfect for sorting the mail and keeping things organized.

OPTION 1:
DAYTIME CASUAL

An affordable way to create a little drama in the entryway: dark paint. By day, it gives a cozy sense of coming home, emphasizing the contrast between the sun outside and the indoor light. The light/dark dichotomy goes even further here, as this entry opens to sun-filled living and dining rooms.

What is the first thing you'd like to see when you walk into your home? The wall opposite the front door is the ideal canvas for something affordable and attention-grabbing. This is a great place to get a little extravagant—even expensive wallpaper is affordable in small doses. Here, a bronze alligator pattern framed by smooth, dark walls adds texture and sheen.

For organization lovers, this entry is a veritable feast: A cherry-veneer console has not one but two shelves, plus drawers for closed storage. Rattan baskets in two sizes keep the shelves neat. The top, too, helps you get it together: A wooden letter stand and brass pharmacy lamp let you sort mail right there. A dish catches car and house keys. A tray holds papers or letters that need to accompany you out the door. And on the wall above hang two pretty-as-pictures bulletin boards, fabric-covered, with frames stained to match the console.

OPTION 2:
GLOW IN THE DARK

A change in furniture and accessories turns the entryway into an especially elegant space in which to greet guests.

Here, a long, curving mahogany console table has a shelf that doubles the display space for collectibles. The alligator wallpaper glows in the candlelight, as do metallic accents ranging from the oval mirror in a bronze frame to the polished-nickel ferrules that cap the slender round legs of the console.

Height variances keep the eye moving over an almost symmetrical arrangement of accessories, as does the mix of materials—silver, bronze, and glass, all reflecting the light. On the shelf below, a stack of books topped by a multifaceted crystal sphere echoes the shape of the mirror above. We took the dust jackets off the books to reveal their beautiful hard covers.

THE PERFECT PIECES FOR YOUR ENTRYWAY

It doesn't take all that much to create an entryway that helps you get out of the house on time in the morning and makes you glad to come home at night. These items will get you there.

First impressions happen here. So make the entry welcoming.

— Bob Williams

TABLE

- Try a console, a narrow table that is designed to be set against a wall. In minimal space, this white lacquered demilune table gracefully gets your attention, especially against a dark wall.
- A petite pedestal table between two chairs or a slim desk with drawers would work just as well.
- In a large entryway, a round table is a classic choice.

SEATING

- A chair by the door gives you a place to put down packages while you take off your coat.
- A settee, like the rattan one above, looks inviting. At parties, it can be a place for guests to put handbags or briefcases.

ORGANIZERS

- End last-minute key searches: Choose a pretty bowl and commit to dropping your keys in it.
- Include a basket, tray, or letter stand for mail and papers that need to go out.
- Don't forget about hat and glove storage, an umbrella stand, and a coatrack or hooks.

RUG

- Make sure your front door can open over the rug and that the rug stays in place to avoid slips.
- A round rug can define a space. Runners can warm up hallways or stairs.
- If you have young children, you may prefer durable flooring that's easy to clean and mats inside and out to wipe feet.

ART + ACCESSORIES

- Make a personal statement with a favorite piece of art or a collection of family photos.
- Introduce pops of color with a few well-placed accessories.
- Bring a bit of the outdoors inside this transition space with some greenery—branches from your yard can work—or fresh flowers to greet guests.

LIGHTING

- A lamp on a console is welcoming at night and uses less energy than an overhead fixture.
- If you don't have a high ceiling, try a combination of a pendant mounted flush with the ceiling and wall sconces.

STYLES YOU CAN LIVE WITH: MIRRORS

Mirrors in an entryway can do so much. They can function as:

- A place for a last-minute glance before you head out the door. And guests appreciate a place to check their appearance when they enter.
- An inexpensive alternative to artwork. You can even take frames you find at a flea market and mount mirrors from a craft store in them.
- Part of a wall arrangement with photos and art.
- A way to visually enlarge an area, add interest with what they reflect, or brighten a dark space.
- Wall decoration that many people find easier to match to their furniture than artwork.

BE OPEN TO OVAL

An oval mirror is a smart buy: Its pretty shape and simple frame make it a shoo-in for repurposing. And it can be hung vertically or horizontally.

FIND THE RIGHT ANGLE

A wide wood frame can read traditional or modern, and a classic rectangular shape complements most consoles and chests.

GO ROUND

Almost 3' across, a mirror this size, with a geometric pattern, can be the focal point of an entry.

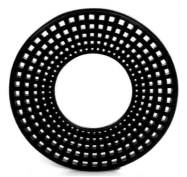

OPT FOR OCTAGONAL

Hand-applied silver-leafing gives a French antique feel. Dark distressed trim helps link the mirror to wood furnishings in a space.

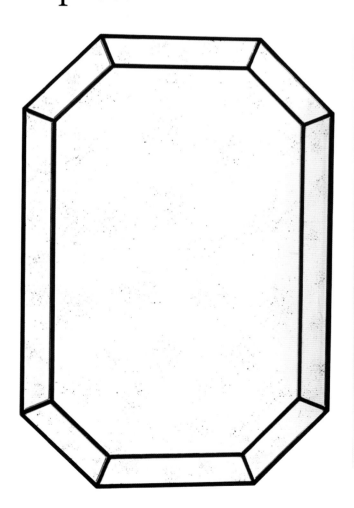

GEOMETRY LESSON

A cutout frame featuring a stylized arabesque pattern in white resin looks great against a dark wall. Hang two side by side for a powerful impact.

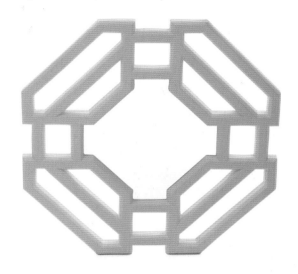

STAY CLASSIC

A combination of clean lines, rich veneers, and classic elements offers a less ornate and more sophisticated way to convey tradition.

EASY MATH FOR ACHIEVING A LOOK YOU LIKE

In order to create continuity, consider which spaces you can see from the entry as you select items for it. While diverse, the pieces in these groups have common threads that can be expanded upon in other rooms. One way to start your equation is to choose a favorite piece and build from there.

An Art Deco–style console with hand-applied silver-leaf (top row) brings 1930s Hollywood glamour home. It can be the centerpiece of a sophisticated silver, black, and gray color scheme with crystal highlights.

A pedestal table (center row) is an entry classic. Simplified details make this one more modern. Flank it with two striped oval-back chairs and add a lamp of handblown glass with a silver lining.

An iconic bench (bottom row) says modern without putting on airs. Pairing it with rattan baguette baskets emphasizes the casual overtones and adds texture. The mirror keeps the look interesting without going overboard.

Art Deco–style console

Squared-off pedestal

Faux-suede bench

 +  +  =

ARTFUL DECO

Reflect light and channel Parisian panache with a looking-glass console, sophisticated gray upholstery, a simple flower arrangement, and wall sconces.

Well-tailored chair   Fresh flowers   Candle sconces

 +  +  =

TRADITION WITH A TWIST

Updated details are the common thread: a table's square pedestal, a chair's striped fabric, a mercury-glass lamp's modern shape.

Fun fabric   Supersized mirror   Silver lining

 +  +  =

CASUAL MODERN

No need to live a hard-edged life: The earth-tone cushion softens the bench's metal base. Shades on the chandelier make it look less severe.

Cylindrical baskets   Cutout mirror   Shaded chandelier

A NEW DAY FOR YOUR ENTRYWAY

BEGIN HERE

We admire the calming, simple glamour of this entryway, with its chocolate-brown walls, mirrored surfaces, and wood floor. However, someday you might want to take it in a different direction— maybe something a little more traditional. The arrangement opposite offers another way to make a dynamic first impression. And any one of the ideas highlighted would add some pizzazz on its own.

FOUR WAYS TO GET THERE

TRADE CONSOLE FOR CABINET: Get more display space and enjoy added drama with the height. The green lacquered boxes inside make great accents and are excellent for hiding clutter.

INSTALL SCONCES: The way you light a space can really transform it. Wall sconces give an intimate feel similar to that of the lamp on the console at left.

PAPER THE "IMPACT" WALL: Wallpapering a single wall is a cost-effective choice. The bamboo motif on the wall opposite the front door welcomes you and brings a sense of the outdoors inside.

ADD A RUG: This one continues the nature-inside theme of the wallpaper with its branch motif. It warms up the space well and makes the entry seem more like a room than a pass-through.

DON'T UNDERESTIMATE THE DETAILS

Accessorizing the entryway gives you one more chance to make it truly practical, hospitable, and personal, as well as connected to the rest of your home. At right are three ways to do that, and on the following pages, a sense of what this trio of additions can do for an entry when put together.

Even without major square footage, the entryway allows plenty of room for self-expression. Add personality with an injection of color, or through paintings or photos in the stairwell, a runner down the hall, or a painted banister. Or place a single folk-art find on a console to introduce a collection in another part of the house.

The entry should allow your guests to get settled and make sure they're looking good. — Mitchell Gold

HAVE A GUEST BOOK

- Introduce a sense of old-fashioned hospitality by leaving a guest book open in your entry.
- Buy one with fine-quality paper and pair it with a great pen. We've been lucky enough to have artistic friends even leave us a sketch.
- A fun idea and useful memory jogger: Take instant pictures and include them with guests' entries.

ADD COAT HOOKS

- Space coat hooks at least 5" to 6" apart to accommodate winter coats.
- They're great even if you have a coat closet, as extra spots for guests' coats.
- Kids seem to be more likely to use them than a closet.
- They can be a fun way to exhibit a collection of hats.
- If you have the floor space, a coatrack is also an elegant addition to an entry.

COMPLETE THE CONSOLE

- Accessories can do double duty: These millinery forms are a clever way to store hats.
- Group three accessories together to create a balanced arrangement.
- An easy way to achieve a pleasing effect is to include one tall, one medium, and one shorter item.
- Over this console, photos with wood frames and white mats work well with warm tones.

GUEST-READY

The pair of vintage millinery forms is unexpected yet practical. We chose simple metal coat hooks to mirror the metal frame of the bench beneath, as well as to avoid overpowering the space and to keep the focus on the console wall. Standard placement for hooks is about five feet off the floor; here they're higher to accommodate the bench underneath. Putting the guest book on the bench gives guests the chance to sit and write a note; at evening's end, it can be stowed in the console drawer.

Head set

Hook up

Memory keeper

THE LIVING ROOM

Whether it's your main gathering spot or the place where you entertain, your living room can be customized to fit all its functions in truly comfortable fashion. We think it should also be designed to convey who you are and how you like to live, because, after the entryway, it's often the first impression people get of your home. Let us guide you in deciding how you'll welcome your guests and make them glad they stayed.

THINGS TO CONSIDER

Here are layout ideas for compact, midsize, and spacious living rooms in different shapes and with a variety of connectors between rooms—open plans, narrow doorways, and wide arches. Remember that if you have a compact room, you can always adapt one of the seating groups from a big multi-area plan.

The layouts suggest solutions to two key questions:

- What will you do in the room? Read, watch TV, entertain—or all three?
- What do you want the focal point to be? Do you want to highlight a feature like a fireplace, a garden view, a prized collection, or a sofa that says come in and sit for a while?

Examining your room from the twin perspectives of form and function is a big help in making it comfortable. And note that the right arrangement is one that makes the most of your space without feeling crowded or difficult to move through.

While some homes have separate living and family rooms, others have a single room that combines the functions of both. Keep in mind that you may also find a layout you like among the floor plans on page 142 in the Family Room chapter.

COMPACT

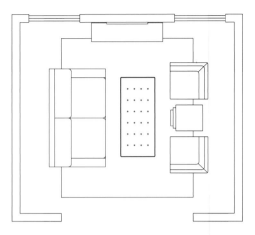

1. CHAT ROOM: This welcoming space calls out for conversation. A settee faces two stylish corner chairs with nesting tables between them. A tufted bench offers a place to set down a snack tray. Between the windows is a slim console with a mirror above it that helps enlarge the space visually.

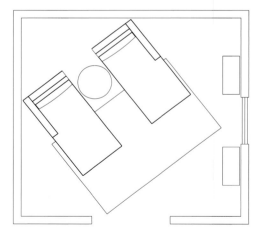

2. READING BUDDY: For a unique and intimate arrangement in a small space, try an inviting duo of one-arm chaises set at an angle. Place a table between them, or push them together for more intimacy. Étagères next to the window can be used to hold reading material and display collectibles.

MIDSIZE

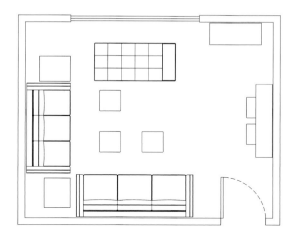

1. DRAWN TO THE VIEW:
When your window frames a beautiful view, keep it unobstructed. A low daybed in front of the window keeps sight lines clear. A bar and a console with ottomans underneath, which can be used as extra seating, make this space entertaining-ready.

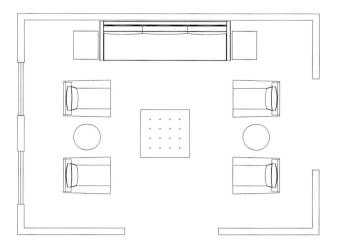

2. AN EYE FOR ART:
When rooms open to one other, they can share a single focal point. Here, art over the sofa could also be the highlight of an adjoining room. Furnishings set symmetrically—a long sofa with matching end tables and pairs of chairs—allow the energy in the space to come from the art.

SPACIOUS

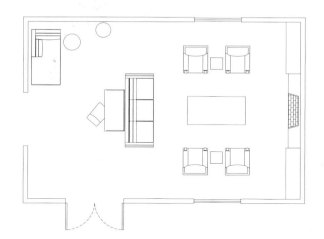

1. FOCUS ON THE FIREPLACE:
A fireplace wall is the focal point in this large room suited to several functions. The seating area is ideal for entertaining. The desk behind the sofa is an appealing place to write, while the chaise is a relaxing spot for reading or enjoying the view.

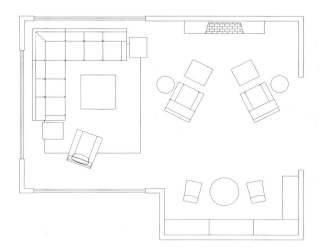

2. LIVE IN A LIBRARY:
An L-shape plan turns a niche into a book-lover's haven with built-in shelves, a round library table, and two chairs. Wing chairs and matching ottomans face the fireplace. A sectional, occasional tables, and a chair, anchored together by a rug, form a third conversation area.

OPTION 1:
DESIGNED FOR DISPLAY

Certain furniture arrangements are just plain useful. For the living room, one of our favorites is a sofa facing a pair of armless chairs. With this arrangement as a starting point, you can use color, furniture, and accessories to create many different looks. To illustrate this, we took a 20' x 30' living room and arranged it twice.

The one we put together here has a soft palette that perfectly suits its primary function—as a beautiful display space for photos and collections. The room's appeal also comes from its faux paneling, an affordable way to add architecture: Wood trim was applied to walls in a square pattern, and then everything—including the wood floor—was painted white to create a serene feel.

1. PLAN IT OUT: Before you lift a thing, carefully plot your layout on paper—this prevents avoidable mistakes.

4. DIVERSIFY: Form an unexpected vignette with a few of your favorite collectibles and a piece of artwork.

2. ARRANGE THE SEATING AREA: Neutral hues on shapely furnishings help modern and traditional pieces blend well. A rich rug defines the grouping.

3. ILLUMINATE: With consoles in place and artwork hung over them, we added lamps with artful and practical qualities that set a modern tone.

5. MAKE IT SPECIAL: To garner the attention it deserves, a collection of handblown glass bottles gets the console all to itself.

6. DO THE MINIMUM: A few details—pillows, a throw, flowers on the coffee table—are all that's needed to finish the space.

THE RESULT: ART AND COLLECTIONS STAND OUT

Arranging pieces you love so they get the attention they deserve makes a room feel personal and unique. And by not overcrowding the room with furniture, you let the eye enjoy each shape.

The room strikes a good balance between showcasing objects and being comfortable for conversation. Adding the tufted chair forms a U-shaped configuration that further facilitates group talk.

The seating area also lets you take in the backyard views. And while the upholstery fabrics are muted, a mix of metallic finishes subtly livens things up.

OPTION 2:
IDEAL FOR ENTERTAINING

To create this look, we started by repositioning the seating area opposite the entrance. You'd be surprised how different you can make a room feel just by rearranging the furniture.

The goal was to create a room that could easily handle a crowd—but without sacrificing coziness on quiet nights at home. The shelter-style sofa with tufted bench seat, for instance, is as good for stretching out on as for seating three.

A balanced arrangement of furnishings and the blue-and-brown color scheme are warm and inviting. Fabrics are soft, good for camouflaging spills, and mostly solid, except for a stripe that picks up the other colors in the room, resulting in a space that's soothing and relaxing for guests—and for you!

1. WARM IT UP: Roll out a textured wool rug that contrasts softly with the white-painted wood floor.

4. MAKE IT WORK: Pedestal tables suit the sofa's high arms. Nesting tables sit between the chairs. A console is useful for serving.

2. SET IT UP: Two striped chairs visually balance the taupe-brown shelter-style sofa opposite.

3. CENTER IT: A rectangular bench ottoman in the middle can be shared by those sitting on the sofa and chairs or serves as extra seating.

5. PERFECT PAIRS: Prints accent the entryway of the room. A lamp with a blue ceramic base adds color, while a white lamp on the table adds a dash of 1960s style.

6. TIES THAT BIND: Pillows and accents visually connect furnishings, including a hall cabinet framed by the doorway.

THE RESULT: SEATING AND SERVING SPACE FOR ALL

Entertaining is easy in this room. You could comfortably accommodate twelve people. Several pieces provide extra seats—a bench ottoman that doubles as a tray-topped coffee table, two kiwi-hued cube ottomans tucked under the console, and an iconic 1960s molded-plastic chair in the hall. Armless chairs are easy to share.

There are plenty of surfaces on which guests can put down a plate or drink, too. White-lacquered nesting tables are used as a side table, making them always ready for company. The console can be cleared of accessories and set up as a buffet.

The layout of the room also aids with large-group socializing. You can go from doorway to seating area to other rooms without walking through people's conversations.

THE PERFECT PIECES FOR YOUR LIVING ROOM

Here are six essential living room pieces and suggestions for what to think about before buying or replacing them.

The living room is often the main place guests spend time and get to know something about you. — Bob Williams

SOFA

- A classic shape and soft solid color will make it—and the room—easier to update with other furniture or accessories.
- Well made means well padded. Grab the arm—you shouldn't feel the wood frame.
- For flexibility, consider a slipcovered sofa and then choose a second coordinating slipcover for a whole other look.

CHAIRS

- Rather than matching them to the sofa, use chairs as an opportunity to add pattern or deep color.
- Choose different types of chairs so all who use the room can sit comfortably.
- Include small pull-up chairs—in a corner, by a fireplace—to bring into a conversation area if you need extra seating.

OCCASIONAL TABLES

- Side tables provide a place for drinks, books, or a table lamp by each chair.
- Drawers or shelves will let you tuck things away—like coasters and cocktail napkins—to keep the room looking neat and tidy.
- Try different styles, each with a visual tie to another element in the room.

RUG

- A rug can define a seating area within the room or, in an open plan, distinguish between living and dining areas.
- Consider picking a rug first and letting it be the inspiration for your color scheme.
- Patterned rugs are pet- and child-friendly, thanks to their stain-camouflaging ability.

STORAGE/DISPLAY

- For a favorite collection, find a special piece to showcase it well.
- Include both open and closed storage—a tiered console behind a sofa, or a buffet cabinet whose top can be a serving surface.
- Besides their practicality, étagères and bookcases have vertical shapes that interact nicely with the room's other pieces.

LIGHTING

- Think of lamps as accessories—both the bases and the shades can bring spots of color to the room.
- Ensure that the shape and visual weight of the lamp—how big it appears rather than its actual size—is in proportion to the table it's on and the sofa beside it.
- Shade height should be at eye level when you are seated, to prevent glare.

STYLES YOU CAN LIVE WITH: SOFAS

You'll spend a lot of time on your sofa, so it's worth analyzing how you want it to function:

- Where in the room will you place it and what size sofa will fit?
- How many will it seat daily? How many when company comes?
- Should it be long enough to lie down on?
- If you sometimes need an extra spot for overnight guests, should you choose a sleep sofa?
- How much use will it get? Does its covering need to be particularly durable?

Also think about comfort:

- Do you prefer loose cushions you sink into or a tight seat and back that make the sofa easier to get on and off of?
- Do you prefer a deep sofa seat? Throw pillows can help people of various sizes customize the depth. With the back pillows removed, a deep sofa can be wide enough for one person to sleep on.
- What arm height is most relaxing for you?
- What fabric or leather covering not only looks good but also feels good to spend time on?

Here are several sofa styles with features that satisfy a range of needs. For more on sofas, see Upholstery Talk on page 28.

TODAY'S CAMELBACK

A tight back offers support, especially when angled to suit your own back. Round bolsters can serve as armrests, while high sides add a protective, cozy feel.

NAP-TIME NIRVANA

Easy elegance: The plush cushions, 8' length, and low roll arms to rest your head on all encourage relaxing. Classic details like a kick-pleat skirt take it uptown.

MODERN SPACE-MAKER

Armless sofas look slim but sit big—a plus in small spaces. Use pillows to add comfort. Tall legs make a sofa look lighter and seem to take up less room.

SAY IT WITH LEATHER

Leather gives this square-arm mid-century modern sofa sleekness and richness that set the tone for a room. A tufted back shows off the leather's character.

CLASSIC UPDATE

Low pleated English arms combined with exposed wood feet instead of a skirt look fresh. Three cushions mean three people can sit comfortably.

THANK THE BRITISH

This new take on an English Chesterfield has a modern appeal in solid blue. Leaving the seat untufted is less fussy and ups the comfort. Handsome detail: turned legs with brass ferrules.

TIME FOR A CHANGE

Want to update your living room quickly? A slipcovered sofa gives you possibilities. Here we show four different looks with the simple switch of a slipcover, a rug, throw pillows, and wall color. (Painting one wall, rather than a whole room, is another way to make a big impact affordably.) Fresh flowers are optional but always welcome!

1. A soft, tonal look is a great place to start. The dark slipcover looks rich against the pale-blue wall and beige rug. Pattern is restricted to a single pillow for a feeling that is classic and serene.

3. Trading the brown slipcover for crisp white is a great change for spring. The pillows and rug stay the same, but the wall is painted a warm bronze, allowing the white slipcover to really pop.

2. Here, we keep the dark slipcover and blue wall but swap the beige rug for a brighter color-block design and the throw pillows for blue ones that make the look more modern.

4. Who says you can't wear white after Labor Day? The same bronze wall combined with a new branch-patterned rug and taupe-and-green textured pillows easily take the room into fall.

EASY MATH FOR ACHIEVING A LOOK YOU LIKE

Ask ten people for their definition of "modern," "traditional," and "country," and you're likely to get as many different answers. We love to mix and match styles and create new definitions—such as Soft and Modern, Hip Traditional, and Modern Cottage. At right are a few of our easy-to-execute ideas for combining furnishings into fresh versions of these styles.

The soft blue sofa fabric (top row) is a soothing neutral with a little more oomph than beige. Modern wood pieces are stunning because of their simplicity and high-quality materials. Don't be afraid to add a little glitz with a gold lamp.

The blue velvet sofa (center row) is current, with clean lines and brass nail heads, but still traditional enough because of the fabric. The candlestick floor lamp, mirrored chest, and corner chair all add to the graphic, clean look.

The crisp white denim sofa (bottom row) mixes naturally with glass, wood, and broken-in leather. The country-comfort style comes from the curves: plump cushions, the jug-style lamp, the circular tabletop, and the rounded chair back.

Soft seats, sculpted back

Clean and classic

Sleek yet slipcovered

SOFT AND MODERN

Keep shapes simple and colors solid, and add interest by mixing in a variety of textures in the upholstery, occasional tables, rug, and accessories.

Homage to Henry Moore + Warmth of inlaid wood + Sophisticated slipper

HIP TRADITIONAL

Help connect setting and furnishings by choosing time-honored styles with current details and materials.

Candlestick cousin + Stunning sparkler + 17th-century roots

MODERN COTTAGE

Subtracting the froufrou and clutter and limiting the colors and patterns in a room are easy ways to create this style.

Versatile glass + Flea-market find + Old-world comfort

HOW TO DISPLAY YOUR ART AND PHOTOS

Part of making a home truly your own is the addition of artwork and family photographs that tell your story. The color and style of these pieces are also key to warming up a space and ensuring it's a comfort to come home to. Sometimes, all it takes is a single work to anchor a sitting area. Often, photos and art look great grouped together. Here are some examples of how to keep it simple and do it well, plus a few additional tips:

- The center of a piece of artwork should be about 5' off the floor if you have standard 8' or 9' walls, so that you don't have to look up or down to view it.
- Small prints or photos look better grouped together, as do small accessories. If small works include print, writing, or fine details, it's nice to position them so people can view them up close.
- A more affordable alternative to buying a big piece of art for a large space is to fill the space with smaller works. You can start with a few pieces and add more over time. Choose works with a common element—perhaps their subject or their frame style—and make this one of the things you collect in your travels.

HAPPY FAMILY: Unify a mix of snapshots and portraits by putting them all in frames of the same color on a console or buffet.

GIVE PROPS: Rather than hanging art, lean it against a wall for a more casual look that is easier to change and forms interesting overlapping vignettes.

Mix artwork and mirrors in
a gallery-style montage.

A NEW DAY FOR YOUR LIVING ROOM

BEGIN HERE

With a limited color palette, distinctive but classic furnishings, and some advance planning, you can design a room that is both beautiful to begin with and easily added to over time. The room below is a good example. It already has a classic sofa in an eye-catching hue, an appealing mix of shapes and materials, good reading light, and convenient serving surfaces. The facing page shows how any or all of the four elements highlighted can be changed to take it to the next level.

FOUR WAYS TO GET THERE

ROTATE COLLECTIBLES: Display different pieces from your favorite collection, or bring in new items like the blue glass birds on the mirrored cubes to help change the room's color scheme.

SHIFT YOUR STYLE: The antique chair didn't look inviting, so we replaced it with a leather one, which is pretty special too—and more comfy. Its metal frame helps modernize the room. We'd put the wood chair in an entry, where the focus is on style, not comfort.

ADD SHELVES: What room wouldn't benefit from more storage? Think about adding bookshelves in pairs for a balanced look. They also add height, serving as a visual link between windows and furniture.

WARM WITH A RUG: Going from bare white wood to a lush shag rug is a subtle but significant change. It adds texture and helps to define the conversation area.

DON'T UNDERESTIMATE THE DETAILS

We definitely feel we're never truly finished decorating our homes. In fact, we design them to be easily refreshed with the seasons, when life circumstances change, or simply when we feel like it. However, we also know it's important to get a home finished for everyday life, right down to the details, so that it's comfortable to live in and always ready for guests.

A living room needs personal touches to feel truly welcoming.

— Mitchell Gold

ENLIVEN WITH FLOWERS

- Flowers shouldn't overpower a room; keep them small, low, and simple enough to truly be accessories.
- Flowers don't have to cost a lot. A group of three single blooms in separate bud vases of a similar style will have a big impact.
- Sometimes it's enough to bring in greenery from your yard and use jars or glasses as vases.
- Try to buy local, in-season flowers, which are more affordable and feel more authentic.

SHOW OFF KEEPSAKES

- Think about what you'd like to collect or what you already own, and find the right piece of furniture on which to display it.
- Group accessories on a tray for added presence.
- Putting similar items together gives them more power than arranging them separately.
- Items with something in common—color, material, shape—make for cohesive displays.
- Change your displays with the seasons. Start an accessories closet for your rotating treasures.

SPRUCE UP BOOKSHELVES

- Mix the way you arrange your books, stacking some horizontally and standing others upright.
- Get creative about bookends—flea-market treasures can find a home here.
- Round objects, such as vases, sculptures, and crystal spheres, contrast nicely with the angular books.
- Go for some open spaces—give a few large objects shelves of their own. If you find you have more books than you can display, donate some to your local library.

PRETTY AND PERSONAL

Symmetrical arrangements of books and accessories are attractive, especially in a pair of backless bookcases placed side by side. The key is getting the right balance—part of the appeal comes from seeing white space around the objects. Near the bookcases, a single piece of art rather than a few smaller pictures keeps the room from looking cluttered. The striking blooms in simple bud vases add a nice pop of color. An early twentieth-century botanist called flowers "sunshine, food, and medicine for the soul." We concur.

Highlight collections

Shelve symmetrically

Brighten with blossoms

REVITALIZED RANCH

You don't need a cottage to create a house that feels like a country home for your family. This standard one-story 1960s ranch is a cozy getaway for family, friends, and dogs.

Owners Nick Bewsey and Nelson Zayas lived in the house for a year, getting to know the space, before working with an architect to make renovations. The setting—a six-acre property in rural Bucks County, Pennsylvania—was the impetus for the biggest change they made to the house: adding windows and glass doors to let in light and views.

The furnishings blend pieces from different eras. Soft color and pattern entice but don't overwhelm. Carefully curated collections like the wall of group portraits in the dining room are warm and personal. Several rooms feature wall-to-wall wool sisal blend, a natural fiber that's both forgiving of spills and dog-friendly; it's clear that kids and pets are welcome here.

With many collections on display, the house is a continuing channel for the creative expression of its owners, who also extend their passion for decorating to their work life: They run a design business called Skylark Interiors, in Ottsville, Pennsylvania.

PREVIOUS PAGE: Gray walls and white-painted floors make the dining room feel slightly different from the rest of the house. To avoid competing with the wall of photos, the patterns in the room—on drapes, the area rug, and a pendant lamp—are all in the same color family. A cabriole-leg table, with a base painted like the floor, works nicely with more modern chairs in short white slipcovers.

OPPOSITE: "We wanted a guest bedroom we'd feel comfortable sleeping in ourselves," says Nick. "It looks out on the garden, so we kept it neutral overall and spiced it up with reds, oranges, and browns—all colors found on the property." Slipcovered in matelassé, the bed feels homey and romantic and complements the garden view. Wood blinds can block out all light to encourage guests to sleep in. Antique Thebes stools with concave tops look like they belong in a garden, and the cutouts make them appear to take up less space.

RIGHT: An antique red-painted side table contributes to the overall color scheme. The bottom shelf is a neat spot to store magazines.

BELOW: The floor plan shows where Nick and Nelson added windows and doors to the front and back of the house in order to let in more sun and views.

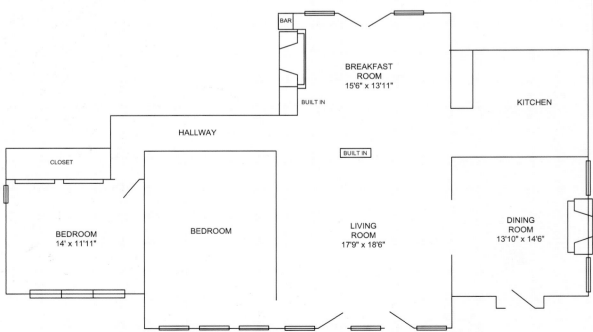

BAR

BREAKFAST ROOM
15'6" x 13'11"

BUILT IN

KITCHEN

HALLWAY

BUILT IN

CLOSET

BEDROOM
14' x 11'11"

BEDROOM

LIVING ROOM
17'9" x 18'6"

DINING ROOM
13'10" x 14'6"

OPPOSITE: A stay in an old hotel that featured a circle of chairs where guests lounged in the lobby was the inspiration for this breakfast nook. It makes a cozy spot for a casual morning meal.

ABOVE: Built-ins help keep the house organized and uncluttered. In the sitting area, a bar, left, and wood storage (with the family pup, English bulldog Dash, standing guard), right, are highlights of the paneled fireplace wall.

LEFT: White china, a pressed-glass vase of flowers, and vintage wood. Timeless.

RIGHT: Nick and Nelson collect the letter "N." This alabaster piece is one of their favorites.

BELOW RIGHT: Between the sitting area and living room, a wall of CDs is more than it appears: "A collection doesn't have to be objects. It could be your art books or, in Nick's case, jazz CDs," explains Nelson. "We had this built-in made for his collection because his CDs are something that defines him. They should be visible, not tucked away in drawers."

OPPOSITE: A wheeled pallet from the 1930s becomes a coffee table that doesn't need coasters, and it's wide enough to hold books and dinner plates. A 5' x 8' polka-dot wool rug unifies the diverse pieces.

FOLLOWING PAGE: Even though the house has an open floor plan, where one room leads to another, it still feels cozy. The key is creating a balance by filling your home with the collections you love without letting things get cluttered. Nick and Nelson have managed to do it perfectly.

CHAPTER 4

THE DINING ROOM

For many of us, decorating the dining room is a process filled with anxiety-inducing questions. Do you want it to be formal, with a crystal chandelier or a china cabinet? Does it sit empty except at the holidays? How do you carve out a space for a dining room if you're working with an open floor plan? Creating a homey dining space doesn't have to be stressful. Ask yourself, "What will make family and friends feel welcome here?" And don't be afraid to consider using your dining room for purposes other than entertaining, such as a home office, library, or gallery. Our favorite use of the dining room, however, is for memorable family meals or a romantic dinner for two.

THINGS TO CONSIDER

Most dining rooms include a table, chairs, and a china cabinet or buffet. However, the room size and shape, the style and placement of the furnishings, and the art and accessories leave plenty of opportunity to personalize the room.

If you have a home with an open plan or an expansive doorway that shows off the dining room from an entryway, take into special consideration the flow from room to room, as it might influence how you place the furniture. When you begin decorating, make sure to choose furnishings and accessories that have a unifying blend of colors and styles to create a cohesive feel.

You should also consider ways to get more use out of the space. You can give it a dual purpose by using it as a library or home office, or you can simply make it so inviting and efficient that you'll want to use it much more often than for holiday feasts.

Here are some floor plans in three general room sizes to help you consider how to place your dining-room furniture. They offer ideas of how to make a big room feel warm or a midsize room do double duty. They also include examples of both small and large dining areas that open directly to living areas.

COMPACT

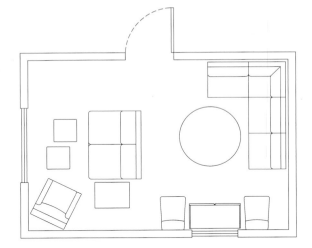

1. **BUILD IN:** A banquette and space-saving pedestal table in this small, open living/dining area offer a cozy place for a relaxing meal. Hinged seats provide discreet storage space, while a shelf mounted to the wall can be used to display photographs or collections. A chest by the window lets you stash even more; chairs on either side stand ready to pull up to the table.

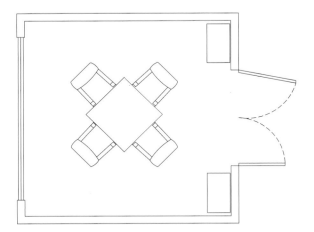

2. **FOUR SQUARE:** Symmetry has a calming effect, especially in small spaces. This space feels intimate and boasts the ultimate in comfort—upholstered armchairs all around the table. Narrow consoles by the door provide serving surfaces without interfering with people's movement around the room.

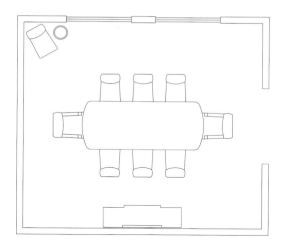

1. IN THE MIDDLE: A long dining table with eight chairs is the focus of this room. The table's rounded edges contrast nicely with all the straight lines. A mirror over the buffet reflects light from the windows opposite. A small, round accent table by an armless chair can be moved near the larger table to hold wine or ice.

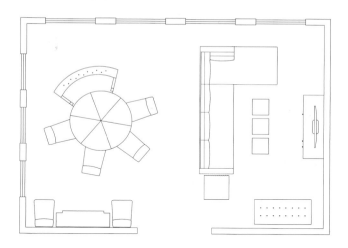

1. HOMEY HOLIDAY DINNERS: Keep it casual with this open-plan dining and family room. Kids can be excused from the table to watch a movie on the sectional, while parents can linger and still keep an eye on them. For bigger crowds, the table can be expanded and the two extra chairs added to it.

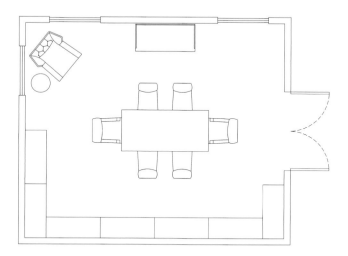

2. READ WHILE YOU EAT: A combination library and dining room lets you make more use of a space. Bookcases line the walls. The table can be used both for eating and for spreading out to work on a project. There's a reading corner as well as a decorative desk—you can borrow a chair from the table to sit at it.

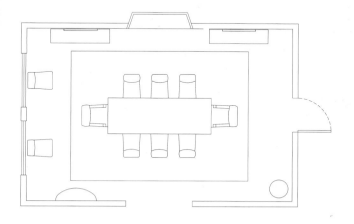

2. ALL THE BELLS AND WHISTLES: Double your storage and display space with matching sideboards flanking a fireplace. Art over the hearth is visible from the doorway. A rug adds warmth, while a circular bar and demilune console add curves. Additional chairs by the windows offer more seating options.

OPTION 1: SOFT AND MODERN

What style of furniture and accessories will give you the dining room you want? Here are two looks for rectangular dining rooms. The first we call Soft and Modern, and the second, Hip Traditional.

To us, modern doesn't mean hard-edged. And what better way to express this than with round pieces—a pedestal table, a pendant lamp, and a curved dining bench. Also contributing to the softness are upholstered seating, which offers the benefit of introducing warm and friendly hues into the room; the loosely gathered pale-blue linen drapes; and a wall covered in grass cloth that adds a nice texture. Watch us put the room together step by step, at right, then turn the page to see how all the elements create an up-to-date eating and entertaining space that expresses modern comfort, both visually and physically.

1. CONSIDER THE ARCHITECTURE: Plan how much furniture to use and where to put it so you can still appreciate the tall French doors and warm-toned grass-cloth wall.

4. MAKE IT SYMMETRICAL: Center a pedestal table under the lamp, place a buffet between the sets of doors, and add two chairs to balance the bench.

2. START WITH SOMETHING SPECIAL: Bring in a curved dining bench. Both its color and its shape will contribute to making the room unique.

3. GO BIG: Center a large pendant lamp in the room. It feels more modern than a chandelier, and its simplicity won't detract from the rest of the furniture.

5. DRESS THE WINDOWS: Hang drapes that emphasize the height of the French doors. (Have someone hold the ladder.) Their classic gathered style can read modern or traditional.

6. ACCESSORIZE, ADD FLOWERS...AND EAT: Keeping accents simple—a centerpiece on the table and only a few items on the buffet—allows you to admire the furnishings' beautiful wood grain.

THE RESULT: COMFORTABLY CURRENT

The outcome is our sense of modern: warm and welcoming, more mid-century than Euro-stiff. The soothing colors and plush seating emphasize the soft in our Soft and Modern style, and there's no sacrifice of comfort for looks. The round table, curved bench, and comfy upholstered chairs form a cozy eating area that's great for conversation.

Open shelves make the buffet against the wall appear lighter and allow the grass-cloth wall covering to peek through. The table's richly grained ash veneer is the focal point; its round shape showcases the wood beautifully. Its 60" top and pedestal base make it possible to pull up an extra chair or two for company. In addition, it's an extension table— always a good investment. With the leaf in, it can seat eight. Extra chairs could be placed on either side of the buffet and in the corners of the room so that they're always on hand when needed.

OPTION 2:
HIP TRADITIONAL

If you love traditional furnishings but don't want a room that's formal or stuffy, the look we put together here may suit you.

Go with pieces that aren't too ornate. For example, we chose a table and buffet in book-matched mahogany veneers that convey Georgian elegance but also have clean lines. Instead of a large china cabinet, a buffet with a mirror above it can make a space feel more open.

Fabrics also encourage a relaxed mood: soft blue faux suede on the chairs that's easy to spot-clean, airy white cotton draperies, and the table runner's bright pop of color. Another laid-back element: the flexibility offered by an extension table. This one seats six comfortably; with two leaves in, capacity doubles. Turn the page to see the full reveal.

1. CONSOLE YOURSELF: Sometimes you simply fall in love with the classic lines of a piece and the rest of the room falls into place from there.

4. SET UP THE SEATING: Bring in a double-pedestal table and curved-back chairs updated with tapered legs instead of turned ones.

2. THREE'S COMPANY: If you plan to have a long table, try a pendant trio. Polished-nickel trim and drum shades feel modern.

3. THERE'S A PATTERN HERE: Roll out an area rug. This one brings soft color and subtle texture to the mix.

5. DISTINGUISH WITH DETAILS: Introduce roundness with a mirror and a dash of bright color with a runner.

6. SHARE A COLLECTION: Turn the table into a display space by arranging glass candlesticks and obelisks on top.

THE RESULT: CASUAL ELEGANCE

Sometimes it's the surprisingly simple details that nudge a traditional room forward in time. Here are several that, without shouting, put a twist on tradition:

- Polished nickel, rather than antique brass, for the nail heads on the backs of the chairs and the drawer knobs on the buffet.
- A distressed-silver-and-black-resin mirror frame, rather than the expected wood or bronze.
- A single variety of flower in glass cylinder vases, as opposed to a mixed bouquet.
- Three pendant lamps instead of a single chandelier.

THE PERFECT PIECES FOR YOUR DINING ROOM

Serving, storage, seating, and lighting, plus accessories and art to make the space more personal, contribute to a delicious mix in the dining room. Here are six ingredients to help make it happen.

Our goal is to create a room in which guests will want to linger at the table for hours. — Bob Williams

TABLE

- Round tables can be conversation boosters. A 5' round seats six comfortably. A table with a pedestal base lets you squeeze in a few more.
- Rectangular tables are usually about 3' wide. A 6' length accommodates six people; an 8' length, ten.
- A table with extension leaves is always a good bet. Round tables expand to attractive ovals.

CHAIRS

- Upholstered dining chairs are our favorites. You can't beat the comfort, and they can be used as extra seating in living areas.
- Measure your table before choosing chairs. Standard table height is about 30", so seat height should be 19" to 20", allowing at least 10" for your legs underneath.
- Slipcovered chairs make updating affordable. With washable fabrics, spills cause less stress.

BUFFET

- Open and closed storage in a buffet—shelves and cabinets or drawers—is a useful feature.
- If you don't have a china cabinet, hang shelves over your buffet to showcase pieces you love.
- Consider alternatives to a buffet, such as a low glass-front bookcase, which has modern appeal, or a family-heirloom chest with lots of storage, which makes a room look less matchy-matchy.

LIGHTING

- A chandelier can feel updated without shades.
- Fabric-covered pendants can introduce color and pattern. They're less formal and more affordable than a chandelier.
- Don't forget to shed light on your artwork.
- Consider an alternative to the multi-armed chandelier. For instance, a long rectangular hanging fixture can spread light the length of a table.

DISPLAY CABINET

- Ensure the size and heft of the piece is in keeping with the scale of your dining table so the room doesn't seem out of balance.
- Make sure the piece isn't too big for the room. All that wood can feel heavy and make a room seem overcrowded.
- Introduce a piece that relates in style to your table and buffet but isn't part of the same collection, to give the room an eclectic feel.

MIRROR

- Center a mirror over a buffet and flank it with wall sconces to add sparkle to a room.
- In a small dining room, consider propping a wood-framed floor mirror against a wall to make the room appear bigger.
- Create an arrangement on one wall of a number of small, different-shaped mirrors set in antique picture frames.

STYLES YOU CAN LIVE WITH: SERVERS AND STORERS

Pieces like these can make entertaining easier and ensure your dining room is a wonderful place in which to spend time. A few things to remember:

- It should go without saying by now that measuring is key when buying big pieces, as is making a list in advance of what you need to store and display.
- You should avoid overcrowding the room with furniture. (This is good news, as the dining room can be one of the most expensive rooms to furnish.)
- Invest in pieces with quality finishes. Finishes should have depth, and the wood grain should show through clearly.
- The straighter the lines of a piece, the more imperfections will stand out. As with leathers, distressed finishes are easier to live with.
- Fine hardware—knobs, pulls, and handles that feel good, look good, and work well—makes a real difference. And changing hardware—say, from antique brass to polished nickel—is a quick way to update a piece.
- Balance all the wood with smaller elements that lend color, texture, pattern, or sheen. Flank a tall cabinet with colorful artwork. Put antique chairs or additional upholstered dining chairs on either side of a buffet.

GOOD GRAIN

Simple closed cabinetry adds warmth when it features a richly grained finish like this one in quartered mahogany veneer. To create more verticality, top the piece with a vase collection.

GLASS TOWER

A mostly glass cabinet seems to take up less space. Clean lines and minimal ornamentation let collectibles be the focus. A tall, narrow piece introduces a vertical element into a space.

GEORGIAN-INSPIRED

A china cabinet that incorporates architectural details such as a pediment and moldings can add visual interest to a room without trim. Base and top cabinets separate to ease moving.

PERSONAL PUB

Ideal for entertaining: a bar cabinet. A piece like this would make good use of a corner of a dining room—or living room, when you're ready to change things up.

REFLECTED GLORY

A mirrored finish makes a big piece feel smaller and brightens a dark room. Wood trim ties it to other wood pieces. Straight lines tone down glitz. Double doors provide full access to the interior.

TRUST IN TRADITION

Cabriole legs lift this sideboard off the floor so that it seems less heavy. Drawers keep silver organized and ready for use. Perhaps the best reason to include a sideboard: a much-needed surface for serving.

EASY MATH FOR ACHIEVING A LOOK YOU LIKE

Have some fun with your dining room. Use pieces in unexpected ways. Go for less formal versions of your favorite styles to make the room as relaxed as possible. At right we share three options for creating rooms that are eclectic but cohesive.

Selecting a table and sideboard that match (top row) helps keep things serene. It also lets the open-back chairs, the bright pendant, and your colorful collectibles take center stage.

The four-column pedestal table (center row) and serpentine-front chest have rich finishes and brass details in common, while the dining chair's ferrules and nail heads have the same finish as the lamp.

In this upscale version of traditional country, the cabriole-leg table (bottom row) becomes less fussy when paired with camelback chairs in a simple solid fabric. Polished-nickel knobs dress up the chest.

Simple and stylish

19th-century Empire

Cabriole leg

SOFT AND MODERN

Upholstered dining chairs help put the "soft" in Soft and Modern. Solid-colored fabrics and clean-lined pieces also define our kind of modern.

Bare midriff   Bright spot   Storer/server/stacker

HISTORY HARMONIZED

Elements from different centuries can form the most wonderful mixes—as long as you don't overdo it. Limit the number of pieces and keep them simple.

Deco-licious   Candlestick style   18th-century Americana

DRESSED-UP COTTAGE

All this adds up to an elegant way to do country, right down to the Tramp Art–style lamp, which is more elaborate than the typical cottage craft.

Camelback   Hobo high art   Stately stance

A NEW DAY FOR YOUR DINING ROOM

BEGIN HERE

We've come up with several fun ways to give a dining room a completely different look. While we loved the crisp blue, white, and beige color scheme of the dining room below, we knew the rich grain and finish of the table would look fantastic against a natural-toned palette. We wanted to bring out more of the wood—and provide more storage space. On the opposite page, we got our wish. Note that any of the four updates shown would make a good starting point for the transition.

FOUR WAYS TO GET THERE

WALLPAPER ONE WALL: We fell in love with the grass cloth—it's what inspired us to change. The wall alone makes the room warm and sophisticated. Two simple prints, instead of the plate collection, allow the grass cloth to stand out.

SLIPCOVER YOUR CHAIRS: White denim is great; it can be machine-washed and spots can be bleached out. These slipcovers are tailor-made for the chairs.

CHANGE CURTAINS: The benefits of simple panels: They're more affordable to change and are a great way to inject new color. Store the classic white ones till your next redo.

BRING IN AN ARMOIRE: Quartered mahogany veneers make this cabinet a rich focal point that also offers plenty of storage. Consider moving the console (that was previously against this wall) behind a living-room sofa for more display space or to an entry with a mirror above it.

DON'T UNDERESTIMATE THE DETAILS

The dining room can feel a little static until you personalize it and give it real atmosphere. The trick is to do so without making it look fussy or cluttered—especially on days when it's full of people and platters of food. Too much stuff can make guests worry they might break something.

Some simple final-touch suggestions: Candles give a room instant atmosphere. Everyone looks good in candlelight. And you can save energy! The dining room is also ideal for displaying collections, whether in a cabinet, on the table, or on the walls. Consider, however, making it a collection of fewer, larger items to keep the ambience serene. And it's always fun if those items have a practical side for occasional active table duty, whether as serving dishes or containers for floral centerpieces.

CONSIDER CANDLE SCONCES

- Electric sconces are most easily added during construction, when wiring can be put in walls, but candle sconces can be added any time.
- There are styles for every taste, from classic lanterns with votives to modern taper holders.
- A pair of sconces nicely balances a single piece of art or a mirror over a mantel.
- Shop at antique stores or flea markets for ones that can lend unique personality to your room.

SIMPLIFY THE CENTERPIECE

- We think it's very important to keep centerpieces low so they don't overwhelm the table and impede conversation during dinner.
- Think of flowers as a finishing touch, not a focus. Here we went with one variety of flower in one color.
- White flowers are always a good choice.
- We've seen some pretty convincing "pretend" flowers lately. There are times when they would make life easier...

STACK THE STANDS

- These are wonderful to collect—but it's good to consider where to put them before you start acquiring.
- Everything looks more elegant on a plate or cake stand—even donuts!
- The stands can be more than servers. They make great seasonal centerpieces with displays of candles, fruit, pinecones, or other natural objects or collectibles.
- The stands fuse elegance with homeyness, a welcome combination in the dining room.

READY TO SERVE

The mirrored candle sconces on either side of the vertically hung octagonal mirror create beguiling symmetry. Their reflective backdrops also enhance the candles' glow. We especially like the centerpiece idea: peonies with clipped stems floating in a footed glass bowl. (This is a great way to rescue flowers starting to droop in a vase.) The silver plate stand brings welcome height to the table. And when serving buffet-style, those simple white cake stands sure look great holding stacks of plates.

Spotlight on dessert

Sparkle power

Centerpiece extraordinaire

CHAPTER 5

THE FAMILY ROOM

When you get the family room just right, it can literally be
a reason to stay home. In fact, redoing the family room can
be the ultimate *staycation*. Here, we offer ways of creating
harmony among family members with rooms that are as
good for being together as they are for doing your own
thing. We've found that how you arrange the furniture can
have a real impact on your home life. One of our favorite
ways to get connected: sinking into a cozy sectional in front
of the hearth, electronic or otherwise. A setup like this
might even help you keep better track of your teenagers.

THINGS TO CONSIDER

Whether your family room is big or small, rectangular or square, open to the kitchen or tucked away in the basement, there's a floor plan to help it meet your needs.

Begin by taking out the list you made in Chapter 1 of all the activities your family room needs to accommodate, and compare it to the solutions these plans offer. Of all your rooms, this one may need to handle the most tasks, so scan all of the plans for suggestions on furnishings that can do double duty, like a sofa that's a sleeper or an upholstered ottoman that can serve as either extra seating or a tray-topped snack spot.

Also review the plans to see which pieces you would like as the focus of the room. If, for instance, your goal is to create a welcoming haven that will encourage your kids to invite their friends over, having a sectional and flat-screen TV as the focal points may draw them in.

For more layout options that can suit any type of gathering place for family and friends, please also see the plans in Chapter 3: The Living Room, on page 80.

COMPACT

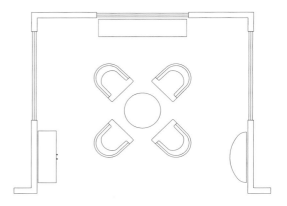

1. SUNROOM/GAME ROOM: Tub chairs hug a round table in a TV-free spot that encourages conversation and card playing. Open to the living room, the layout allows more space for entertaining. Windows on three sides bring in light. Shelves and consoles provide storage and display space.

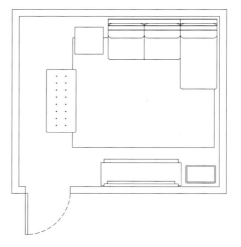

2. MEDIA- AND GUEST-FRIENDLY: Watch TV on the L-shaped sectional. Keeping the area in front of the sectional clear makes opening the bed easy. The bench ottoman is multifunctional, providing both seating and storage space. The console keeps media neat, while a basket can hold extra pillows. A rug ties the whole room together and encourages people to relax on the floor.

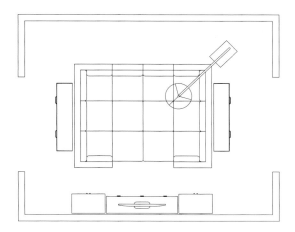

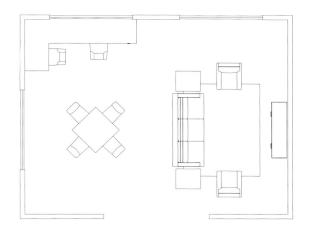

1. EVERYBODY IN THE PIT: This 1970s modular sectional is perfect for cocktail parties, the ultimate family movie night, or a sleepover. To finish the room, add a pair of consoles—here, nicely framed between the doorways—a standing arc lamp, and a media center for the TV flanked by two étagères.

1. WORK AND PLAY STATIONS: The room is open to the kitchen, making the table convenient not only for crafts but also for eating, watching TV, and playing games. A built-in desk forms a homework center in a corner. A rug defines the seating area. This layout allows for smooth flow to all areas of the room.

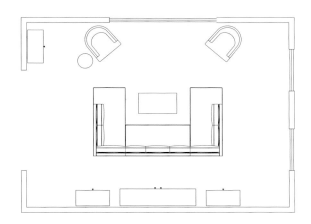

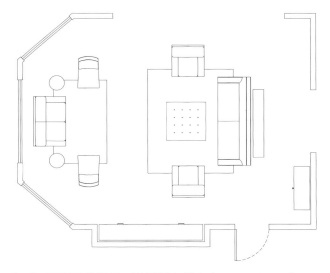

2. ART OF CONVERSATION: Sectionals are a great way to bring people together. The U shape means two people can stretch out, or you can seat a crowd. A small cocktail table fits nicely in the center. Two chairs provide a firmer seating option to those who need it. Storage space abounds here.

2. ENTERTAINING OPTION: This large rectangular space features two seating groups defined by area rugs. An ottoman centers a group including two facing chairs and a sofa with a console behind it. A more compact grouping of a loveseat and two smaller chairs fits nicely in the windowed bay. A corner of the room accommodates storage.

OPTION 1:
MADE FOR MULTITASKING

Here we offer two ways of arranging a large family room. The first shows a serene way to accommodate a lot of activities, while the second puts the focus on media.

Creating a multifunctional room is all about planning. It starts with your list of what activities will go on there. This means paying attention to the layout so that there's room for each activity as well as for traffic flow. It requires measuring carefully to ensure the major pieces needed for each activity—a sofa big enough for snoozing, for instance—will fit, and that there's enough storage for all the stuff these activities might require—CDs, books, craft supplies.

For a busy space like this, a balanced arrangement of furnishings should be a top priority. It provides a sense of calmness even when a lot is happening at once. Choose only a few colors and use pattern sparingly. Finally, add details like pillows, art, and accessories, both to make each area as useful as possible and to link them all together visually. On the following pages, you'll find a family room that can do it all. At right, see how we created it, layer by layer.

1. START THE CONVERSATION: Put down the rug and position the sofa between the windows. (It's a little early to take a break!)

4. TABLE IT: Use side tables in similar sizes but different styles at the ends of the sofas to create balance and add interest.

2. BALANCE THE "BONES": Place a matching sofa opposite the first and center a square upholstered ottoman between them.

3. BOOST SEATING CAPACITY: Add an armless chair at one end to form a conversation-friendly U-shaped seating area.

5. ADD A READING CORNER: Find a chair that sits big yet has a small footprint, and a stool that can double as a side table.

6. SET UP A HOME OFFICE: Arrange a desk, chair, lamp, and bulletin board in a niche to make the most out of this space.

THE RESULT: ROOM TO RELAX, ENTERTAIN, READ, AND SURF

An abundance of seating—and a variety of seating options—lets the space suit small- and large-group activities well. Pattern in a mostly solid room has a lot of visual weight—here it helps the armless chair hold its own with the cream sofas but is otherwise confined to pillows to keep a potentially busy scene serene. Outfitting a home office with furnishings that enhance the room's aesthetic helps it blend right in.

Making use of the entire space, including corners, allows for more activities. Yet the room isn't over-furnished; it takes into account people needing to walk around and kids wanting open floor space in which to play.

OPTION 2: DESIGNED WITH MEDIA IN MIND

Our goal for a media room: to give everyone a comfy seat and clear view of the screen—plus a place to prop feet and pillows to curl up with, making movie theaters unable to compete. And even at home, no show is complete without snacks, so we made sure to place serving surfaces within easy reach.

Sectionals are a great seating choice here, and there are as many shapes as there are room layouts— L shapes, U shapes, ones that incorporate chaises and sleep sofas, and even full "pits," as you can see in one of the family room plans on page 143. There are also modular types—composed of armless chairs, for instance—that can form a unique configuration sized to your particular space. Because they use smaller units, modular sectionals offer the bonus of being easy to take with you when you move—and to arrange differently in your new space.

1. SEAT A CROWD: Arrange an L-shaped sectional in front of the wall you've designated for the TV.

4. STORE MORE: Use an étagère as a place to counter all the technology with family photos or mementos that can warm up a room.

2. AND ADD SPACE FOR ONE MORE: Put a comfortable leather club chair across from the sectional.

3. BRING ON THE ENTERTAINMENT: Add a console with shelves for media components and space for the flat-screen above.

5. LAYER IN LAMPS AND TABLES: Be sure there are places to put popcorn and a light for reading movie reviews.

6. END WITH ACCENTS: Use pillows and accessories to balance the dash of color provided by the ottomans.

THE RESULT: TRUE VIEWING COMFORT

The room not only has furnishings ideal for lounging but also appears comfortable visually. It features a color scheme that won't distract from the action on the screen.

Think about window treatments—this is a good place for blackout shades or drapes, which will prevent glare on the screen in daylight hours.

Consider upholstery fabric carefully—remember the importance of picking something durable, designed to make wiping up spilled food or drink easier.

The layout for the room is a plus: The sectional fits the space without overwhelming it; there's room to pass on all sides. The étagère and consoles—one for the TV and one behind the sofa—allow for storage and display.

THE PERFECT PIECES FOR YOUR FAMILY ROOM

Incorporating these types of furnishings into your family room will help you create a fantastic gathering place that can handle multiple functions with ease. Here are tips on selecting each.

We want to create cool media rooms. I'm from Jersey, and I still don't want a Sopranos-*style setup.*

— Mitchell Gold

SECTIONAL

- Carefully plan the configuration to make the best use of your space. Would an L-shaped, U-shaped, or pit-style arrangement work best?
- A slipcovered sectional can be a good investment; rather than replacing this large piece, change its cover.
- A compact modular armless sectional can be adjusted to fit just about any space.

CHAISE

- Create an oasis of calm in a corner of a busy family room with an inviting chaise plus side table and lamp.
- Chaises come in styles ranging from traditional to modern, shapes including armless, one-arm, two-arm, and even as part of a sectional.
- Try two one-arm chaises with a small table in between as a spot to talk or watch TV together.

COFFEE TABLE

- Leave 18" between table and sofa for maneuvering. Height-wise, 17" to 19" is standard; higher can be good if you're planning to eat on it.
- Consider an upholstered ottoman as a substitute for a traditional wood or metal coffee table. It makes a fine footrest, extra seat, or serving surface (with a tray on top). For young children, it's a safe alternative to sharp-edged wood or metal.

CONSOLE

- Great for a media-focused family room. Mount your flat-screen TV over it; store components inside.
- For media storage, get a model with adjustable shelves, precut holes for electrical cords, vented back panels, and drawers or shelves for DVDs.
- Flank a console with two tall étagères or bookcases to create a stylish wall of storage.

DESK

- Help the room do more: A desk can be a homework station or the heart of a home office.
- Choose a desk with drawers and shelves and have more storage nearby so the top stays clear for use by more than one person.
- A spacious table and chairs might also be a good option, as they can function as a place to do school projects, play board games, or eat a meal while watching a movie.

FLOOR LAMP

- For a light that is especially good over a sectional, try a floor lamp with an adjustable arm (as above).
- A large sectional may benefit from standing lamps at each end.
- A low floor lamp should be at shoulder level. Lamps with adjustable bases let you get the light just right.
- A tall floor lamp should be about 18" behind or beside your reading material to illuminate it.

STYLES YOU CAN LIVE WITH: CHAIRS

Once you have your sofa, complement it with a range of seating types. Here are some options to consider:

- Choose chairs in several sizes and support levels so people of different heights and ages can find something that feels good to them. For example, if your sofa is made for lounging, have some chairs with good back support.
- Keep throw pillows on hand so people can customize chair depth for themselves.
- Consider not only the physical size but the visual weight of a chair compared with your sofa—do the proportions and color look right? For instance, paired with a beige sofa, a dark chair will get all the attention; use pillows to add color to the sofa and help balance the room.
- Enhance interest by mixing in an unusual antique chair or a reproduction of an iconic modern chair.
- Because a chair is less expensive than a sofa and thus easier to replace, consider being freer with your color and fabric choices. A chair's smaller scale also makes it a better candidate for trying a bold pattern.
- In the family room, durable fabrics are great stress reducers, and today there are many options available. Leather can be a good choice, especially the pre-distressed kind so that you're not worried about scuffs and scratches.

PRETTY PULL-UP

The benefit of a full-size chair in a compact footprint: You can carry it where needed—that's why we call them pull-ups. It's a good candidate for room changes, and it also works well beside a bed.

MODERN LEATHER

The square-arm leather club chair is an icon, representing modern with a capital M. Its size allows it to hold its own with a large sofa or sectional. In a big room, two side by side make a dramatic statement.

STRETCH OUT IN STYLE

In addition to the obvious comfort factor, a piece like this enhances a room with graceful lines and tufting, which creates a subtle pattern. Place it where you can enjoy its undulating profile.

WING IT

So civilized...a wing chair makes the perfect place for coffee or cocktails. Modernize this blast from the past with a solid fabric. Nail heads lend a graphic touch.

BEAUTIFUL BARREL

Add a round shape to all the straight lines. Barrel chairs hug you. They are attractive from all angles, allowing them to be placed anywhere in a room. They're elegant in leather, fabric, or a combination of the two.

SLIP INTO A SLIPPER

Great in twos: a duo of these forms an armless loveseat. This piece can be modern or old-school, depending on fabric and leg style. Semi-attached cushions sit well.

CLASSIC CLUB

Restful and relaxing—pair it with a matching ottoman and make it a preferred spot for curling up. With roll arms, welting, and a simple skirt, its casual-traditional look transcends trends.

EASY MATH FOR ACHIEVING A LOOK YOU LIKE

You want your family room to be comfortable without sacrificing style. Here are some ideas for blending furnishings that will help you achieve that goal, in looks from modern to traditional. These equations are both practical and pretty.

Looking like a prop from a 1950s TV set, the modern sofa (top row) has a comfy seat and back cushions. So does the chair, another Ike-era icon in textured fabric that's nice to the touch. The blue vase and tripod table inject appealing roundness.

A linen slipcovered sofa (center row) is in good company with baskets in honey-colored rattan, a weathered gray tabletop of salvaged elm, and bronze cotton velvet on a chair.

Starting with the red tufted-leather shelter sofa (bottom row), these pieces are timeless, each a beauty in its own right. Even though each references a different era, together they create a sophisticated, eclectic mix.

Seats three

Relaxed slipcover

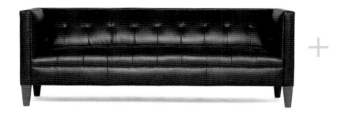

Leather shelter

EASY MODERN

The sum of these pieces is a truly homey look that also has tremendous style—just what you want for a family room.

Scandinavian simplicity + Round tripod table + Square club chair

CASUAL TRADITIONAL

Natural materials and earthy colors predominate. Though new, the pieces share a laid-back, family-heirloom quality.

Textured catchalls + Reclaimed wood + Tufted velvet

CLASSICS COMBINATION

In a room with neutral walls and flooring, the straight lines and rich colors of these pieces allow them to work together despite their diversity.

Mid-century chest + Metal-edged + Updated with pattern

A NEW DAY FOR YOUR FAMILY ROOM

BEGIN HERE

As inviting as the room below looks, we know there will come a time when we're ready for something new. Sometimes it helps to take a step back and envision what's missing before starting your new look. Here we felt it was color, so we injected a few warm hues. The picture on the opposite page shows the same room with four elements updated. Depending on your budget, you could enjoy results from one change or invest in them all.

FOUR WAYS TO GET THERE

FRESHEN UP YOUR ACCESSORIES: A new lamp (or lamp shade), pillows, a few prints, and you're on your way. This doesn't have to be all about new purchases: Simply moving accessories from one room to another will update both rooms.

SWITCH YOUR SLIPCOVER: Having a second slipcover in a fabric that also matches your décor offers visual benefits and peace of mind: You'll always be prepared for sofa emergencies like spills.

GET MORE COMFORTABLE: Tray-topped, an upholstered ottoman serves the same useful purpose as a wood table. But it's better for putting feet up on—and odds are you won't get yelled at for doing so. It can also provide extra seating.

PUMP UP THE COLOR VOLUME: A bright leather chair can be a new focal point. The strong, sculptural shape of this Hip Traditional wingback, which blends modern legs with a traditional high back, also draws attention its way.

DON'T UNDERESTIMATE THE DETAILS

It sometimes surprises us that after carefully planning the major furnishings, people will pay less attention to the accessories. To get the look you want, it's so important to consider accessories with a critical eye—not only your critical eye but maybe that of a design-oriented and honest friend. Something that makes the process easier: Try living with an arrangement for a few days and then adjust. Especially in the family room, it's great when decorative accessories are also practical, as shown here—beautiful boxes for storage or an artfully framed mirror that also visually expands the room. For tips on arranging accessories, see page 34 in Chapter 1. For ideas on displaying art and mirrors, see page 98 in The Living Room chapter.

ORGANIZE WITH BOXES

- Neatly store TV remotes, reading glasses, photos, or pens to jot down infomercial numbers (wink).
- These can be fun and affordable items to collect in your travels and are a great way to personalize a room.
- Mix antique and modern styles. Stacking boxes of differing shapes adds appeal.
- Place boxes and other accessories on trays to create a statement and make them easier to move when you need a surface for serving.

USE MIRRORS AS ART

- Like artwork, a large mirror can be the focal point of a room.
- Consider what the mirror will reflect—doubling the image of the messy bookshelf opposite won't enhance the setting.
- Smaller mirrors set in old picture frames make great additions to a gallery wall of photos and art.
- Mirrors offer the added advantage of brightening rooms by catching light from nearby windows.

TOSS PILLOWS ON THE FLOOR

- When a crowd gathers, oversized accent pillows can be tossed on the rug or leaned against the sofa.
- For pillows that will be used on the floor, look for durable but soft textured fabrics and generous filling.
- Instead of bringing in a strong color or pattern, try a blend of textures—like raffia and a barely there sage stripe against leather—for a rich mix.
- Big pillows can change the comfort level and depth of a tight-back sofa (one with no loose cushions).

A NATURAL CONCLUSION

This beautiful handmade driftwood mirror makes a statement without overwhelming the scene. Its natural coloring and material work well with the other eco elements, like the raffia pillow, rattan tray, and sisal rug. We included a combination of pillows and lacquered boxes in coordinating hues to help define the soft color scheme. These accents are easy to store and replace with boxes and pillows in different shades that can subtly re-dress the space for another season.

A well-framed mirror

Double-duty pillows

A mix of boxes

FEDERAL BEAUTY

We love the way this two-story Federal-style home—just five busy blocks from the Capitol in Washington, D.C.—encourages a tranquil family life.

Since moving in three years ago, owners Chris Tucker and Chris Lear have made a series of comfort-inducing and cost-efficient renovations that have turned the light-filled house into a gathering place for family and friends.

The house's serenity is due in large part to the continuation of soft, soothing color from room to room. Initially, all the rooms were painted different colors, so applying a coat of off-white to most of them instantly created cohesiveness.

Because the circa 1910 house had been expanded over time, the rooms also had wood floors of varying types. Rather than replace them, the owners applied an ebony stain throughout to remedy color differences. They did the same for the doors, camouflaging style variations with brown paint, which had the added benefit of highlighting the white-painted moldings.

Perhaps our favorite thing about this house is the successful balance between the classic architecture and modern furnishings. To make it work, they limited the amount of accessories, color, and pattern in each room and kept the primary furnishings neutral, allowing their personal touches to shine through.

PREVIOUS PAGE: A view from dining room to living room reveals a continuation of the neutral palette. Complementing the room's original trim is new, slim picture-frame molding—a subtle way to add an interesting architectural element when you have high ceilings. The drapes are semi-custom; each panel consists of two store-bought curtains sewn together.

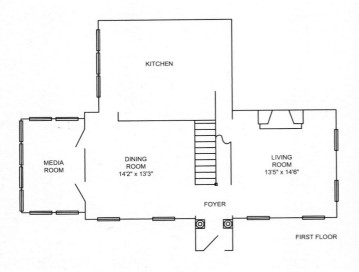

FIRST FLOOR

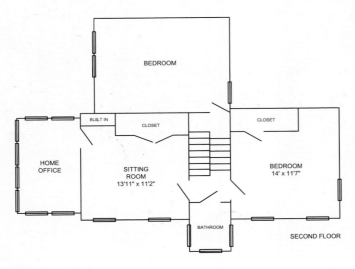

SECOND FLOOR

LEFT: The two-story house has a simple, symmetrical center-hall layout.

ABOVE: A swivel chair with a metal base and warm caramel tufted-leather upholstery fits in with the home's traditional architecture.

OPPOSITE: A transom over the door lets light filter into the family room, where a traditionally styled sofa is adjacent to a pair of modern armless chairs.

OPPOSITE: Textures create richness. A waffle-weave coverlet on the bed nicely contrasts with a shag rug and linen-lined velvet drapes.

ABOVE LEFT: The gray wall behind the white built-in shelves helps the pottery and photographs on display stand out.

ABOVE RIGHT: Using a small chest as a nightstand provides additional closed storage space, as well as surface space for a candle, flowers, books, eyeglasses, and a lamp with a white leather base. The lamp's nail-head trim complements the pattern on the hems of the pillowcases.

TOP RIGHT: A trio of white pottery forms an appealing triangle on the mantel, which is trimmed with classic dentil molding.

BOTTOM RIGHT: Above the fireplace a mirror with a dark cutout frame set against the white wall makes a bold statement. A border of slender picture-frame molding makes the mirror seem grander and unites it with the fireplace below.

OPPOSITE: The living room features elements found throughout the house: ebony-stained floors, off-white walls, original moldings, and simple draperies. A mid-century chest serves as a bar. A white rug looks rich against the dark floor.

FOLLOWING PAGE: The suzani-pattern pillow on the sofa is a strong accent in an otherwise tranquil room. An open-shelved side table and a two-tiered coffee table provide plenty of space for books.

CHAPTER 6

THE BEDROOM

Don't let your bedroom be the last room you decorate. Even if it is a private space that guests rarely see, it is just too important when it comes to quality of life. This is the place that sets the tone for the beginning and end of each day. Is it organized? Is it comfortable? Is it romantic? It should be. This room is truly worth investing in. Here are some ideas for how to create a bedroom that feels relaxing at the end of the day and makes you happy when you wake up every morning.

THINGS TO CONSIDER

Depending on the rest of your living space, your bedroom might have to serve dual purposes, but we think it's very important, whenever possible, to make it a sanctuary. A balanced placement of furnishings will create calm, as will the right amenities for relaxing. For us that means a padded headboard, nightstands on both sides of the bed, a good reading light, and a place to sit.

Depending on your room size, decisions you'll need to make that will determine your layout may include:

- The size of your bed. A king-size can take up a lot of floor space, while a double can feel cramped—which is why queen is most popular.
- The placement of your bed. Would you like it by a window?
- If you have a TV, will it be visible?
- Whether you want some kind of seating. In small spaces, a slipcovered dining chair can be a good alternative to a larger armchair.
- How much storage you'll need. Can some items be kept in an organized closet so the room doesn't feel overcrowded?

Here are six floor plans for different-shaped rooms, grouped by size and designed to get you thinking about the best use of space in your private haven.

COMPACT

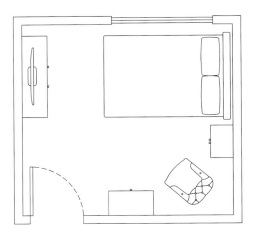

1. BED WITH A VIEW: Put a bed by a wall to save space, or place it by a window to take advantage of a view or breeze. A chest that's tall and narrow allows room for a chair. The low dresser has a flat-screen TV mounted above it.

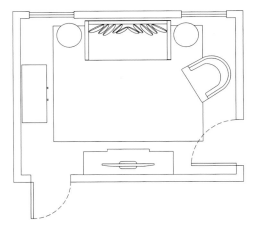

2. SOFA BY DAY: Leave the bedroom look behind until after dark with a daybed lined with throw pillows. A tub chair completes a conversation area defined by a rug. Pedestal tables serve as space-saving nightstands. A dresser offers storage, as does a console with a flat-screen TV over it.

MIDSIZE

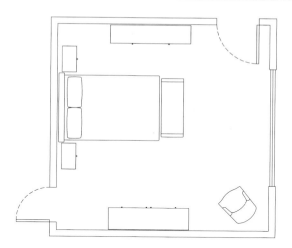

1. ENJOY THE SCENERY: If you have a great view, organize the room so that it offers a few options for taking it in—here, it's a bed with a settee at its foot and a chair in a corner. A pair of dressers on either side of the bed provides plenty of room for storage.

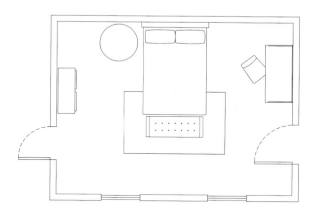

2. WORKING GIRL: Office accoutrements can be stylish enough for the bedroom. Here, a desk and a comfy upholstered dining chair line one wall. A bookcase with closed baskets on shelves keeps work from taking over. A bench at the end of the bed opens to provide even more storage space.

SPACIOUS

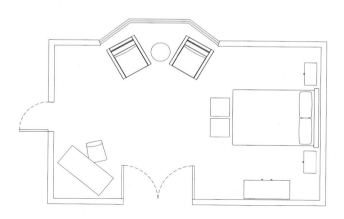

1. SIT/SLEEP/DRESS: Two chairs and a table make a relaxing private spot for coffee. A bed with a tall upholstered headboard takes advantage of a high ceiling and encourages reading. Angling a vanity in a corner gives the beautiful piece presence and softens the lines of the room.

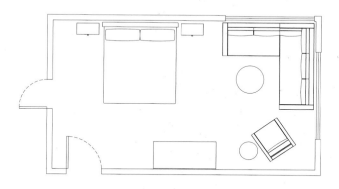

2. SUCH A SANCTUARY: Here, the seating is as luxurious as the king-sized bed. An inviting L-shaped sectional and a club chair for reading fill a windowed corner. Round upholstered ottomans can serve as side tables or a place to prop up your feet. The TV is in an armoire so that it can be hidden when not in use.

OPTION 1: MODERN LUXURY

Here is how our versions of modern and traditional might play out in the bedroom. First you'll see the bedroom in a Soft and Modern style—all the benefits of clean lines without the hard edges. Then you'll see it in a Hip Traditional style—the best of centuries past updated for today. Something we like in both these rooms: The chests, side tables, and mirrors are good investments because they have the potential to be repurposed in other parts of the house—in an entryway, a dining room, or maybe the family room. In the modern sanctuary we put together here, layers of pleasing shapes and subtle colors make it look so inviting you might be tempted to linger in bed a little longer. Turn the page to find the results of all our heavy lifting.

Until you furnish and decorate your bedroom, you'll always feel a little unsettled. — Bob Williams

1. BEGIN WITH THE BED: Plan where you'll position it. Choose one with good center support for the box spring.

4. FINISH THE BED: Layer in luxury—a marble table, round like the mirror, and studded end-of-bed ottomans.

2. TOP THE HEADBOARD: Use a large fish-eye mirror as a focal point and as a sleek contrast to sumptuous white bedding.

3. ADD STORAGE: White drawer fronts on the wood chest visually connect it with the mirror and bed.

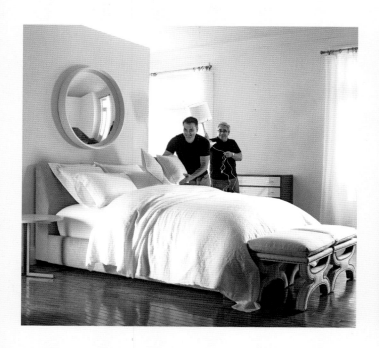

5. LIGHT AND ACCENT: A trim lamp suits a petite table. (Don't try the fake-hitting thing at home.) Two throw pillows are plenty.

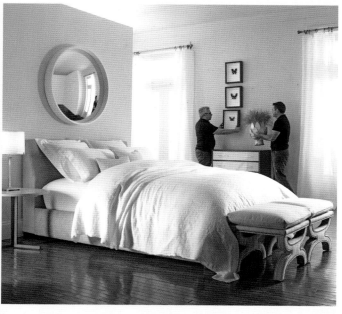

6. ACCESSORIZE: Balance a framed trio on the wall with a tall greenery arrangement on top of the chest.

THE RESULT:
READY FOR RELAXING

This is such a charming mix. Round shapes contrast with the straight lines of the bed and dresser, as does the luxurious but casual bedding, which looks so comfortable. Natural materials like linen on the bed and the stone tabletop work effortlessly with twenty-first-century materials like the resin of the mirror's frame and the lacquer on the wood dresser's drawers. And there's even a touch of tradition added by the X-stretcher ottomans at the foot of the bed, updated with solid fabric and nickel nail heads.

The layout of the room is really practical. Building a half wall and keeping the bed and dresser in one area of the room lets you have both a sleep sanctuary and a second area that can be set up as a home office or gym.

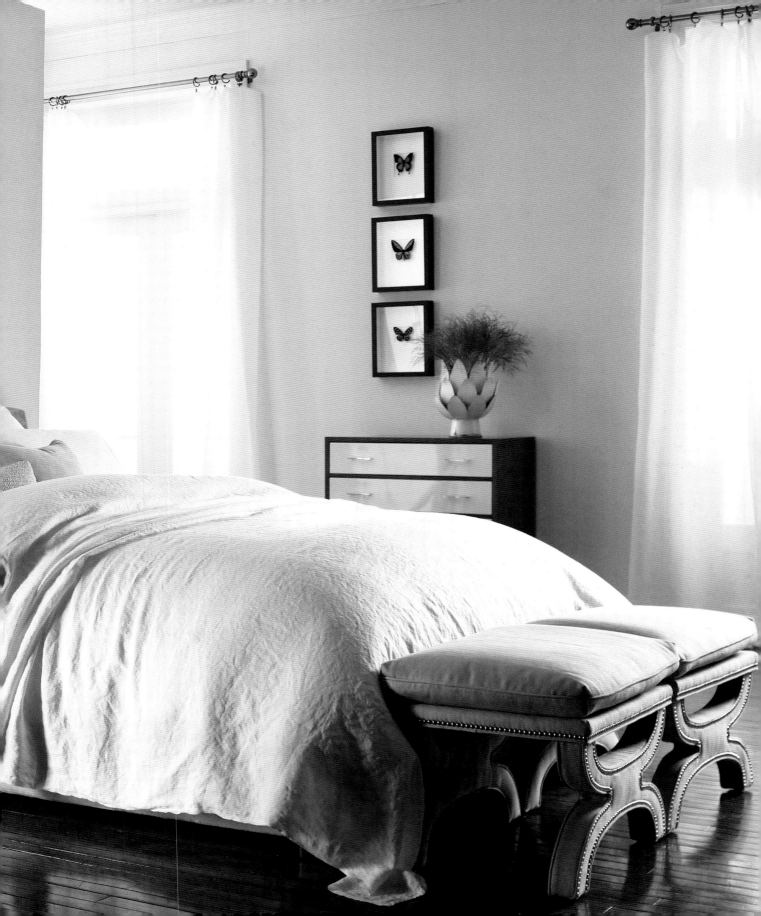

OPTION 2: CLEAN-LINED TRADITIONAL

We're always striving to make a room in which the comforts of the past match the way we live today. Achieving that means paring down the number of pieces, from furniture to accessories. You can get traditional by mixing textures, tones, and solid colors, as we've done here. What defines this space quickly is the choice of bed—both its shape and fabric communicate classic style. In distinctive navy velvet, the graceful silhouette of the curved, sheltering headboard and footboard is a striking focal point. See for yourself on the following pages.

A bedroom should feel sensuous and stylish all at once. Just say no to a lot of pattern—it's too jumpy. — Mitchell Gold

1. BED AS FOCAL POINT: Deep-blue velvet against a pale-blue rug and grass-cloth wall will catch and soothe the eye.

4. LEATHER LOVER: Give the bed a finished look—and yourself a place to sit—with a classic tufted-leather bench.

2. UPDATED ICON: Choosing a pedestal table as a nightstand says tradition, but this one sports sleeker lines.

3. USEFUL AND BEAUTIFUL: A silver-leaf Paris-inspired chest and octagonal Art Deco mirror add unfussy glamour.

5. COLOR CONNECTIONS: A lamp with a dark shade and pillows in soft blue and taupe contribute to the overall tranquility.

6. LAST LAYERS: Add a richly colored and textured throw on the bed and some simple accessories on the dresser to complete the look.

THE RESULT: TAILOR-MADE FOR COMFORT

This version of the room feels a little more formal than the first—but not too much. While the bedding has a crisp look, the bed itself feels sensuous. It looks particularly stunning against the textured grass-cloth wall.

The richly distressed leather on the narrow bench adds a casual element to the room. We also like the bench's practical side—at 18" deep, it doesn't stick out far, so it's easy to walk around.

Here, the half wall might separate the sleeping area from a dressing area. The chest and mirror against the back wall serve as a visual connector between the two spaces, and as a visual midpoint between the furnishings and the tall windows.

THE PERFECT PIECES FOR YOUR BEDROOM

The bedroom pieces are simple, but the styles you choose and the way you combine them make the difference. Here are six important parts of the big picture.

I'm addicted to upholstered beds. There is simply nothing that looks so inviting...and delivers what it promises: comfort.

— Mitchell Gold

BED

- Invest in a headboard to give the room a finished look. We like comfy upholstered ones, tall enough to lean against. They come in an abundance of shapes and fabrics and can be dressed up with welting, tufting, or nail heads.
- A quality mattress is a worthwhile investment.
- Bed size depends on room size and how much sleep space you like. Height-wise, it's all a matter of preference: Do you prefer climbing up or being closer to the floor?

NIGHTSTAND

- For comfort and convenience, keep table height within about 4" of your mattress's height.
- Look for enough surface space to handle all of your essentials.
- Having a drawer or cabinet will help you to reduce tabletop clutter.

END-OF-BED BENCH

- A useful spot to sit and put on your shoes or neatly store decorative pillows at night.
- A bench with a semi-attached top is especially comfortable.
- Ensure you have enough room between it and other furniture to get by.
- If you have the space, a loveseat looks luxe and is the perfect place to curl up with a good book.

CHEST

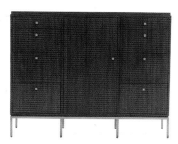

- If you use the top a lot or want to hang a mirror over it, a piece no more than chest-high makes sense. A long, low style works well with a wall-mounted flat-screen TV.
- Can you fit a long, low piece or are two tall, thin chests on different walls better for your space?
- A mix of drawer sizes may be best. Chests like the one above also have a section with shelves behind doors for stacking shirts or sweaters.

CHAIR

- Options for a small room include slipper chairs like the one above, barrel chairs, petite pull-ups, or even an upholstered dining chair, which is also good if you have a desk in the room.
- Don't let the chair become a dumping ground for clothes or for magazines waiting to be read. (Of course, we don't always practice what we preach.)

BEDDING

- A minimal investment to transform your look: Add decorative pillows or get sheets in new colors that work with what you have so you can come up with fresh combinations.
- Layering on textures, while keeping colors soft and subtle, evokes luxury. Try sateen sheets with a nubby knit coverlet or embroidered decorative pillows.

STYLES YOU CAN LIVE WITH: BEDSIDE PIECES

A lamp, a book, an alarm clock, a phone, your glasses, the TV remote, a glass of water, and a few niceties like photos or flowers—where are you going to put them all? Part workhorses and part style-makers, bedside tables contribute big-time to bedroom comfort:

- The style doesn't necessarily need to match that of the bed or dresser.
- You can use two different nightstands. For contrast, put a round table on one side and a chest on the other.
- Drawers or a cabinet let you keep things neat; open shelving gives you display options.
- With a small nightstand, save surface space by installing wall sconces as substitutes for lamps.
- To change things up, consider an exchange with your living room side tables. Or do some creative repurposing: Use an antique wooden stool or a modern plastic chair.

HAVING IT BOTH WAYS

Selecting a nightstand with drawers and a shelf gives you both storage and display space. An elegant piece like this one might make you want to keep things traditional in the bedroom.

SIZE MATTERS

Need more room for your clothes? Try this small chest as a solution. It's a mid-century-modern charmer with fresh white lacquer drawers that also offers abundant space on top.

WEATHERED WOOD

A pale finish like this distressed gray can lighten a room and complement color schemes from blue to brown. While rustic, the finish also approaches modern on pieces with simple lines like this one.

YOUR TURN

It's small, but it sure makes a statement. Glam gold leaf takes a turned pedestal table from traditional to prized possession. Use it in tight bedside quarters now, in other rooms later.

TREASURED CHEST

Take the burden off your dresser by adding precious sweater space in very old-school style. This antiqued eighteenth-century-inspired chest can be a useful nightstand—or living-room end table.

FABULOUS FIFTIES

In addition to having an iconic look and striking blond finish, this unusually shaped piece is particularly practical. It provides double-height surface space as well as a drawer.

STORE IN STYLE

A true friend with benefits in the bedroom is a great-looking nightstand with plenty of storage. This three-drawer chest also offers a top big enough for the necessities and a collection of photos.

EASY MATH FOR ACHIEVING A LOOK YOU LIKE

This is *your* space—make it relaxing and rejuvenating, no matter what your style. Don't limit yourself to matching pieces of furniture—create a very personal mix that truly says comfort to you.

We can't imagine anything more inviting than an upholstered bed. It is ideal for leaning against; it visually softens the look of a room; and it can introduce a soothing color into the mix.

Silver nail heads on the camelback shelter bed (top row) and the bench with X-stretchers are pretty details, further accented by the antiqued "porthole" mirror. A tall, narrow French semainier-style dresser seals the classic deal.

A tall headboard on the bed (center row) is contemporary and romantic. The chest can be used as an extra-large nightstand. The silver-trimmed lacquered boxes and brown velvet bench add to the luxurious look of the room.

Metal details unite the lamp, the bench, and the nightstand (bottom row). White bedding and a white lamp shade...what more could one want? Maybe white drapes and a white rug?

Fit for a queen

Stand tall

Crème de la crème

UNFUSSY GLAMOUR

Classic shapes with historical roots are at home together. Shades of blue mixed with wood and silver create a traditional scheme.

Mirror on the wall   Tall, dark, and handsome   "X" marks the spot

CITY GIRL

Feminine but not frilly, this blend combines practical straight lines with pretty materials in a blue, brown, and silver scheme that is very different from the one above.

Stack it up   Let it shine   Sit pretty

LUXE MIX

Straight lines, low profiles, and muted colors link these modern pieces, each of which has its own quiet yet distinctive style.

Marble base   Warm wood   Metal base

A NEW DAY FOR YOUR BEDROOM

We really liked the bedroom on this page and felt it would take only a few changes to make it a little more comfortable and convenient. The key was to keep the luxurious and relaxing feeling that comes from allowing a bedroom to have room to breathe— leaving some blank space and not over-decorating. On the facing page, the updated version of this bedroom fills in the gaps with a few elegant enhancements.

FOUR WAYS TO GET THERE

HANG DRAPES: Instead of a shade, go with something softer. These warm up the look of the space, introduce color, and filter the light, which can also change the appearance of a room.

RE-PRINT: Arrange a little more art over the bed—but still keep it simple. Instead of a single print, go with a trio that echoes the shape of the headboard.

MIX UP YOUR BEDDING: Another option with big impact. Add a duvet and decorative pillows, and get new sheets that can mix with the ones you already have. This set has a snappy yet subtle detail: a striped cuff that picks up colors in the room.

BRING IN A BENCH: Including a place to sit in a bedroom is an everyday luxury you'll appreciate. The bench is also a great place to put the comforter when it's too hot at night.

DON'T UNDERESTIMATE THE DETAILS

Two big aspects of finishing a bedroom are organizing the little stuff and making the space feel personal. Having places to tuck everyday objects out of sight will help the room look more restful—and give you the space to express yourself without causing clutter. A bedroom can be a better display space for fragile heirlooms or delicate collectibles than high-traffic areas of your home, given the right shelving or surface. It could also be the perfect spot for a wall of vacation photos or portraits of you with your favorite people. The following suggestions will help get the room ready for personalizing.

BOX UP YOUR BEDTIME STORIES

- Putting a basket bedside can be a simple step toward conquering nighttime-reading clutter.
- Woven baskets are a great textural contrast to wood furnishings.
- Consider repurposing a refined-looking linen-covered box or a rough-hewn antique crate as bedside storage.
- Other objects can step in: an old suitcase, an antique chair—the idea is to set up a spot and use it, and then regularly weed out what you've read.

PAINT YOUR CEILING

- A ceiling should be painted first whenever possible, of course, but if you need a quick way to update a room, for a modest expense, this is a way to really warm it up.
- Visually lower a high ceiling with a tone slightly darker than the walls. To make a low one appear higher, go lighter.
- Other options for color or texture overhead include wallpaper, fabric, crown molding, or wood beams.
- Even a coffered, or paneled, ceiling is within reach. A carpenter can build one with standard-size boards and molding.

ORGANIZE YOUR NIGHTSTAND

- Ideal bedside lamps might be decorative as well as functional—they can bring in color and texture. With matching nightstands, try two different lamps that soften the symmetry but still feel balanced.
- Don't overcrowd with knickknacks—leave room for your glasses, an alarm clock, a phone, a water glass, a notepad for 2 a.m. brainstorms, and small luxuries like fresh flowers.
- What better place for photos of your family and friends than your bedside table?

OASIS ACHIEVED

Painting the ceiling blue makes the room feel expansive and adds to the overall mellow vibe. Convenience and beauty reign bedside: A nightstand with lots of surface space is always beneficial—this one even has a pullout tray in case you need more. A drawer provides closed storage, and the shelf gives you a neat spot to tuck a reading-material receptacle, saving floor space. (Measure the shelf before you go looking for a basket to put there.) Along with the ceiling, the bedside lamp also contributes to a blue-sky, desert-country look.

Artfully ordered

Side table storage

Blue skies inside

CHAPTER 7

SMALL SPACES

At times, we've both lived in some really compact spaces—like when Bob first came to New York and made a 4.5' x 10' room at the 34th Street YMCA his home. At other times we've enjoyed the luxury of having small spaces within our homes—landings, nooks, an extra bedroom—to decorate. Our design principles have served us well in both types of rooms. Deciding what functions a room needs to handle becomes especially important when decorating small spaces. Proper storage is also key for avoiding clutter. Using mainly soft, solid colors and a few bright accents promotes calmness. In this chapter, you'll find ideas to help you create beautiful and functional small spaces.

DOUBLE-DUTY FURNISHINGS

For a room that needs to do it all, there are certain pieces of furniture that can make the square footage twice as useful. Here are some recommendations.

Small space doesn't have to mean small style if you outfit it properly. — Bob Williams

SLEEPER SOFA

- When in doubt, give yourself the option of an instant guest room with a sleeper sofa.
- In tight quarters, a chair-and-a-half twin sleeper is an alternative to a larger sofa bed.
- Another option: a sofa with a single bench cushion and loose back cushions that you can remove when using as a twin bed.

DINING/END TABLE

- A round pedestal table, such as this one, can be a great end table for your sofa, providing plenty of room for a lamp, a drink, and a display of family photos. It can also be your principal dining table, or use it as an extra table for dinner parties.
- The round shape will allow you to fit more chairs around the table, so you'll always have room to squeeze in one more guest.

NIGHT AND DAYBED

- This backless piece can feel less overpowering in a small room than a sofa would.
- It can visually divide a space without blocking a view.
- Set against a wall, it can be lined with pillows and function as a sofa; with pillows removed, it can be an additional sleeping spot.

STORAGE OTTOMAN

- Using an ottoman with a hinged or lift-off top as a coffee table lets you tuck things—like kids' toys or extra blankets—out of sight when guests come.
- As an end-of-bed bench, it's a place to store extra pillows. One lined in cedar can store woolens.
- It can help create an entryway: Put it by the door with a mirror above it and store boots inside.

UPHOLSTERED DINING CHAIR

- Upholstered dining chairs are especially good in compact spaces because they can also serve as desk chairs, bedside chairs, and extra living room seating.
- Though small in size, they're nearly as comfortable as occasional chairs.
- Slipcovered chairs look particularly soft and inviting.

NESTING TABLES

- Use a set stacked together as a side table by a chair, and they'll always be handy when you need them for company.
- Separate them and line them up in front of a sofa to serve as a compact coffee table.
- Their design, color, or material can add interest to a room without taking up much space.

GET ORGANIZED

- The key to living well in a compact space is eliminating clutter. Lined with bookshelves, a narrow 2' x 18' strip along one wall offers abundant storage.
- Think twice before installing built-ins. You can take bookshelves with you when you move.
- An easy-to-install floor-to-ceiling curtain on a track hides all and softens the setting.
- A tonal color scheme with pattern only on the petite chair makes the space seem larger.
- The sofa is a sleeper. The lightweight cubes can be easily moved to open the bed, and toss pillows can go into a basket.

WHY THE FLOOR PLAN WORKS: A storage wall keeps home office and dining necessities out of sight so the sitting area stays pristine.

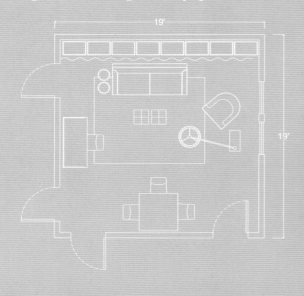

CLAIM A CORNER

- The table is cozy by the window, an ideal place from which to enjoy the light and views.
- An armoire that can hold supplies for entertaining fills a niche nearby.
- The table can also double as a desk, and home office supplies can be stored in the armoire.
- A unified color scheme of warm solid neutrals with highlights of kiwi and red gives the compact space style and serenity.
- A low armless sofa and a tub chair have small footprints. Along with the metal-framed ottomans, they help make the space feel more open.

WHY THE FLOOR PLAN WORKS: The sofa provides a low, unobtrusive divider between the two areas and helps delineate the traffic flow from one space to the other.

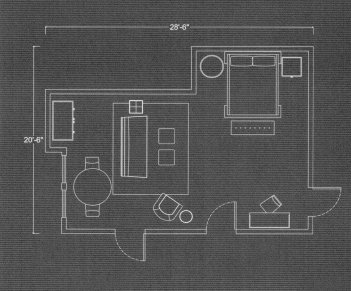

USE IT WELL

- Measure carefully before selecting furnishings for landings or nooks so that pieces don't stick out into walkways.
- A few special furnishings, like this sleek daybed and colorful, shapely side table, can make use of a landing by turning it into a cozy reading spot.
- The same setup paired with bookshelves could turn an extra bedroom into a library.
- These spaces are also great for showcasing art or a family heirloom. Hanging or leaning a piece against a colored wall and lighting it properly will bring the appropriate attention to it.

WHY THE FLOOR PLAN WORKS: The daybed's long, narrow shape nicely fills the landing without interfering with passage up and down the stairs.

MODERN COTTAGE

To Amanda Seitz, snug square footage does not mean sacrificing style—or lifestyle. She had several goals for her 1,025-square-foot home, an updated 1960s Connecticut bungalow. It had to be easy to maintain, showcase her collections, and accommodate overnight guests. And she wanted it set up quickly so she could live comfortably and be ready for company.

These photographs were taken only six months after Amanda moved in, and we admire her commitment to getting everything unpacked and decorated with such speed. The results are lovely: a smart mix of antiques, new pieces, and favorite collectibles she had always wanted to display. The key to success, according to Amanda, a twentysomething first-time home buyer: "I chose to buy a smaller home so I would have more time and money to decorate it the way I wanted."

While Amanda did decorate quickly, she has been collecting and thinking about what she likes for most of her life. She grew up in her family's business, J. Seitz & Co., a home furnishings shop in New Preston, Connecticut, where today she is the jewelry, clothes, and gifts buyer. This foundation helped influence her casual but elegant style and made decorating her bungalow much easier.

PREVIOUS PAGE: Amanda considered putting twin beds in the guest room, but they would have taken up all the space in the room and then she wouldn't have been able to use it herself. So she opted for a chair-and-a-half that opens to a twin sleeper and added shelves so that the room also functions as a library.

ABOVE LEFT: Zebra print, a favorite of Amanda's, makes only brief appearances (including on a vase on the dresser) to keep the calm room from looking busy.

ABOVE RIGHT: The poufs are easy to move when opening the bed. They also make good coffee tables for those who have children, because there are no sharp edges.

OPPOSITE: Amanda chose the bed—with a tall tufted headboard and upholstered rails instead of a traditional footboard—because of its romance and glamour.

RIGHT: On the first floor, an open-plan living and dining area helps make the compact house feel more spacious. Upstairs, an interior window in Amanda's bedroom lets light pass into the room from the hallway, and its window ledge also serves as a nightstand.

OPPOSITE: Compact but comfortable, this symmetrical conversation spot in the living area features armless chairs in linen and a square side table with a shelf for books. A trio of blue-and-white patterns—on the throw pillows, Oriental lamp, and graphic rug—delineates the color scheme.

BELOW: Amanda shares her home with her four-year-old long-haired Chihuahua, Riley.

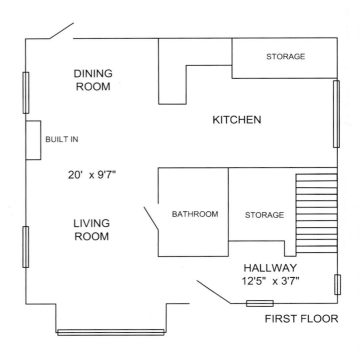

DINING ROOM

STORAGE

KITCHEN

BUILT IN

20' x 9'7"

LIVING ROOM

BATHROOM

STORAGE

HALLWAY
12'5" x 3'7"

FIRST FLOOR

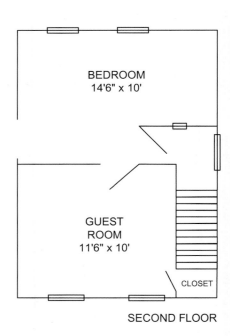

BEDROOM
14'6" x 10'

GUEST ROOM
11'6" x 10'

CLOSET

SECOND FLOOR

ABOVE: Seashells placed on a glass-topped coffee table with a driftwood base speak to Amanda's love of nature. In addition to shells and sea fans, she also collects nests, bones, and skulls.

OPPOSITE: The dining area's unexpected mix includes a petite wood pedestal table and see-through wire chairs that appear to take up less space. A serpentine-front chest is modern in metal. The octopus triptych, a print divided into three parts that were framed separately, is a great focal point. A leather mirror hung from a peg reflects light from the glass-paned door.

FOLLOWING PAGE: We love the prewashed white denim slipcovers on the sleeper sofa and large ottoman in the living room. The look is timeless, and the washable fabric, which gets softer with each wash, is especially pet- and guest-friendly. On the wall, Parisian platters and a ceramic deer head Amanda found at the famed Brimfield flea market in Massachusetts stand out against beige walls and complement the upholstery, built-in shelves, and trim.

PARIS HOTEL STORIES

Gourmet Shops of Paris

ANNIE KELLY ROOMS TO INSPIRE IN THE COUNTRY

ANNIE KELLY ROOMS TO INSPIRE

Octopus - Gamochonia

INDEX

CREDITS

All photography by Michael Bruton/Innovations Imaging and styling by Kevin Hertzog unless otherwise noted.

Melanie Acevedo: pages 16, 23, 35, 106–115, 164–173, and 208–217. Styling by Kim Ficaro.

Antoine Bootz: pages 45–57. Styling by Kevin Hertzog.

Sally Fanjoy & James Labrenz: pages 30–31.

Courtesy of Mitchell Gold + Bob Williams: pages 5, 9, and 10.

iStock: pages 15, 17 (left) and 43 (left column, all).

David E. Brown: page 17 (right).

A special thanks to Frette at ABC Carpet & Home in New York City for loaning us the beautiful bedding on pages 182–185, and to Lee Jofa for the Cole & Son wallpaper on pages 62–65 and 73, and the Mulberry wallpaper on pages 75–77.

Thanks also to ABC Carpet & Home, Aero Studio, and Mantiques Modern in New York, and to Windrose Antiques, Jules Antiques and Fine Art, and The Farmer's Wife in Greensboro, NC.

Melcher Media would like to thank David E. Brown, Amélie Cherlin, Daniel del Valle, Barbara Gogan, Coco Joly, Lauren Nathan, Holly Rothman, Jessi Rymill, Robert Swanson, Alex Tart, Shoshana Thaler, Anna Thorngate, Rebecca Wiener, and Megan Worman.

ACKNOWLEDGMENTS

Books are always a team effort. We were so lucky to lead a team of people who share our style sense and dedication to making your home a place of peace and comfort.

Particular thanks to Mindy Drucker, who stewarded this project through with wit, patience, and an uncanny ability to know how to communicate as we do. She is a writer, sister-in-law (to Mitchell), and supporter of equal rights for all. Thanks also to Lia Ronnen, executive editor and project manager, and Lindsey Stanberry, project editor, at Melcher Media—two of the most positive, caring, and talented people we know—as well as Charles Melcher, Kurt Andrews, and the other members of their team. They were an incredible joy to work with.

Our special thanks to editorial director Doris Cooper and the Clarkson Potter team, for appreciating our style and helping us share it with readers.

Thanks to book designer Naomi Mizusaki, for helping us make all this information easily and beautifully accessible; stylist Kevin Hertzog, for being so talented and so fun to work with; stylist Kim Ficaro, for her great eye; stylist Gail Gardner, for her insider's scoop on where to get great stuff; photographers Melanie Acevedo and Antoine Bootz, for their very pleasurable tours of the Homes We Love; the team at Innovations Imaging, in Greensboro, NC—Michael Bruton,

Aaron Bulla, Joe Garrett, Wynn Myers, and Rick Penland—for their speed, professionalism, and knack for making us feel at home; and the home-owners who opened their inviting houses to us: Amanda Seitz, Nick Bewsey and Nelson Zayas, and Chris Tucker and Chris Lear.

Thanks to our wonderful MG+BW team, especially Roger Turnbow, go-to guy for insights into how best to show our style; Charley Holt, Chris Jennings, Nathan Banks, and Ryan Levy of our amazing marketing department, ready at all hours to find photographs, offer ideas, and provide support; Carl Marmion, for his incredibly swift execution of some really great floor plans; Eloise Goldman, who's been getting the word out about our new book since we first mentioned writing it; visual merchandisers and stylists extraordinaires John Zisel and Brent Sheffield; Nan Huegerich, legal expert and new mom; and everyone who pitched in on the day-to-day tasks so we could do this, including George Ackerman, Dan Gauthreaux, John Bounous, Dan Swift, and Tommy Davis, with us in PD from the start and retired this year.

To our partners, Tim Scofield and Stephen Heavner, who make us comfortable and still love us despite all the late nights and the Blackberrying in the middle of everything, as well as the rest of our families for their support of all we do.

2 1982 02403 9038